Scrapbooking for Profit

*Cashing in on Retail, Home-Based,
and Internet Opportunities*

REBECCA PITTMAN

ALLWORTH PRESS
NEW YORK

08 07 06 05 04   5 4 3 2 1

Published by Allworth Press
An imprint of Allworth Communications, Inc.
10 East 23rd Street, New York, NY 10010

Cover design by Derek Bacchus

Interior illustrations by Rebecca Pittman and Jeff Newman

Interior design by Mary Belibasakis

Page composition/typography by Integra Software Services, Pvt. Ltd., Pondicherry, India

ISBN: 1-58115-406-2

LIBRARY OF CONGRESS CATALOGING-IN-PUBLICATION DATA

Pittman, Rebecca F.
   Scrapbooking for profit: cashing in on retail, home-based, and Internet opportunities/Rebecca F. Pittman.
      p.   cm.
   Includes bibliographical references and index.
   ISBN: 1-58115-406-2 (pbk.)
1. Selling—Scrapbooks.   2. Scrapbooks—Equipment and supplies—Marketing.   I. Title.

   HF5439.S38P58 2005
   381'.45745593—dc22

                                                                    2005011202

Printed in Canada

Table of Contents

Acknowledgements

So much goes into writing a book that it is hard to separate the elements of creative support and pragmatic contributions.

Many wonderfully talented people gave of their time and effort to make this possible.

I would like to thank Jeff Newman for his indispensable help with the illustrations that head each chapter. Jeff is an enormous talent who not only supported me throughout the writing of this book, adding insight and making sure the cartoons "popped" with his great eye for detail, but also took his time away from other graphic design projects to do so. Thank you Jeff . . . you are deeply appreciated, and the most consistent of friends.

The time and talents of the following people are so warmly acknowledged: Ann Kingrey of Get Gone Cruises, a scrapbooking cruise company with a huge heart for causes. Jacque at Camp Crop, a mountain retreat for the scrapbook enthusiast. Russ Williams at Invention Home, the one-stop shopping Web site for patents and inventions. Russ, your enthusiasm for your project is well founded! Michele Gerbrandt and Debbie Mock of *Memory Makers* magazine for their invaluable help. Penny McDaniel of Legacies, a scrapbooking store in Loveland, Colorado. Penny gave so unselfishly of her time in allowing me to peek behind the scenes of a scrapbook retail store. Thank you, Jeanne Maire of Your Crop Shop in Arvada, Colorado, for your time and insight into retail scrapbook stores. David Kovanen, president of Addicted to Rubber Stamps and Addicted to Scrapbooking. David spent a copious amount of time informing me of the pros and cons of running an Internet store. Thank you so much, David. Don Meyer, Director of Marketing and Public Relations of the Craft and Hobby Industry, gave me pages of statistics on the world of scrapbooking. Thank you, Don!

David Sutphin of Dream Maker Software showed me the amazing new world of computer scrapbooking and his wonderful site, *www.coolclipart.com*.

Janel and Sandy at the Paper Attic in Sandy, Utah, for their time in answering my questions about retail setup.

A huge thank-you to Suzi Moran, Sharon Colasuonno, Kelly Rice, and Susie Monaro of Creative Memories. They not only graciously showed me their home-based businesses, but they also offered me referrals to their satisfied customers, invited me to crops, and sent me volumes of information on the largest scrapbook franchise in the world, Creative Memories. Much success to you all! And to Cheryl Lightle, President and Cofounder of Creative Memories, for her generous contributions to this book.

Brandi Ginn from Colorado, a talented scrapbooker who turned her love of the art into a productive career, writing and submitting artwork to scrapbook magazines and books.

Jacob G. at the Microsoft Business Solutions Retail Management System Corporation for his input on point-of-sale solutions for new businesses.

As always, I want to thank Nicole Potter of Allworth Press for her invaluable editing of these pages. Nicole always takes my efforts and polishes them into something I'm proud to be a part of. Thank you for your humor and patience, Nicole.

To Michael Madole, Tad Crawford, Derek Bacchus, Jessica Rozler, and all the people at Allworth who took their time and talent to make this book what it is, I say a heartfelt thank you! What a joy to work with you!

There are numerous others who slipped me an anecdote, added a sideline, or put me on the path to information I needed. Thank you so much for caring about the outcome of this book.

On a personal note, there are the people in my life who make me passionate about being here. My four gorgeous sons, Mike, Brandon, Casey, and Ryan, and my beautiful daughter-in-law Janel, make my heart sing and fill my days with laughter and spontaneity. I love you! To Gary—you always manage to be there in your own way. Thank you.

My mother, Collette Wells, who has been my inspiration since I could hold a pen or a paintbrush: I love you, Mom. No one had a better mentor, and I was lucky enough to grow up around your positive attitude and your "never say die" mentality.

My brother Mike, and Vicki, Gloria, and sister Marlena . . . thank you for being there for me and making me feel important. You are so valued—you have no idea!

Introduction

I grew up in Salt Lake City, Utah, surrounded by craft shops, boutiques, and hobby stores, all calling enticingly to the artisans, crafters, and homemakers wanting to add beauty and enchantment to their lives, and in some cases, extra income. Being a craft nut myself, I found this to be a haven of ideas, materials, and information on every craft project imaginable. Next to my mother and the mountains, those stores are what I miss most about Salt Lake.

The Mormon heritage, with its emphasis on genealogy and crafting, has turned Salt Lake City into the scrapbooking capital of the world. It does not surprise me. I've witnessed the attention to documenting one's ancestors in the Mormon Church since I was little. The Family History Library in Salt Lake City is unequaled. You can access it at *www.progenealogists.com*. When you add this to the plethora of stores bulging with decorative materials for every scrapbooking whim, you come up with the recipe for some pretty amazing albums.

It was growing up surrounded by this atmosphere—coupled with the huge burst of interest in scrapbooking in the past few years—that lead me to write this book. In its pages, you will find everything you need to know to start your own business in this fascinating and pragmatic world of documenting and savoring one's memories. Whether you're wanting something small and cozy from home or you're dying to see your name emblazoned on a backlit sign above your shop door, you'll find the necessary information here, from taxes to advertising; setup to inventory; opening to expansion.

I wish you a world of discovery and the perseverance to see your dreams come true!

CHAPTER 1

The Lucrative World of Scrapbooking

The popularity of scrapbooking continues to rise by leaps and bounds, according to Don Meyer of the Hobby Industry Association. "People all over the country are gathering their most precious memories—their photos—and transforming them into creative masterpieces. By adding stickers, decorative papers, rubber stamps, ribbons and a plethora of other embellishments, simple photos become scrapbook pages that last a lifetime. As such, there is an entire day dedicated to the craft." Scrapbook stores nationwide participate in National Scrapbook Day on Saturday, May 1, of each year.

NOT JUST PASTE AND SCISSORS

What started out as a trend has turned into one of the country's most popular craft activities. Each year, the Hobby Industry Association (HIA) puts on the largest craft and hobby trade exposition in the world. "In 1998, there was no scrapbooking on the show floor. However, in 2004, 50 percent of the show floor was scrapbooking," Meyer continues. "It is now a $2.5 billion dollar industry that shows no signs of slowing down."

With the above statistics, it is easy to see that what started out as a means of cataloguing photos in an effort to get them out of boxes and into some form of organized collection has turned into a multibillion dollar industry in just a few short years.

Without question, Salt Lake City is the scrapbooking capital of the world. Scrapbooking combines the Utahan's love for crafts and genealogy. The first rumored enhanced scrapbooks were accredited to women from the Utah area as far back as the late 1800s. It was in 1987, however, that the scrapbook trend became a full-fledged cottage industry. That was when a Minnesota businesswoman, Cheryl Lightle, and Montana homemaker Rhonda Anderson founded Creative Memories, the first company to offer direct-to-consumer photo-storage information, products, and hands-on assistance. This company now boasts thousands of consultants around the world who are teaching people how to organize and responsibly store their photos and memorabilia not only in imaginative, creative ways, but with revolutionary products that preserve the treasured photos for generations to enjoy.

The urge to collect mementos and display them is not new. People have been making scrapbooks for generations. The photos and memorabilia were originally affixed to pages with scotch tape, rubber cement, and glue—even flour paste. With the influx of new camera technology that bombards us today, people are taking even more photos and finding that preserving them in creative albums is not only rewarding, but has created a legacy to pass down to family members who follow—and so much more.

Journaling along with the photographs has become a way to experience and preserve memories. According to Kelli Rice, a Creative Memories consultant, "Our goal is to preserve the pictures as well as the stories that go along with them in order to create a family heirloom."

An excerpt from a 2003 speech given by Cheryl Lightle, Cofounder of Creative Memories, highlights the value of scrapbook albums:

Albums dignify and honor those we love—and heighten our understanding both of them and of ourselves.

Albums communicate with our loved ones at a distance.

Albums celebrate and validate human lives.

Albums help us remember the life around the photo.

Albums capture the quiet glory of ordinary moments that define our existence.

Albums can help us all understand life.

She went on to say, "The passion, the detail, the stories that are captured on our pages are a celebration of all that we love and value."

Recent events poignantly reveal the importance of having a reliquary for family memories. With the passing of President Ronald Regan, a spotlight has fallen on the Alzheimer's disease and its degenerative properties. Creative Memories, in conjunction with its mission to preserve the past, enrich the present, and inspire hope for the future, has partnered with the Alzheimer's Association to raise money and awareness for this important cause.

"Remembering the past helps to define us," states Creative Memories. "People afflicted with Alzheimer's disease are robbed of their opportunity to reminisce—their memories essentially stolen by the disease. Published studies show that scrapbook photo albums enhance the well being of both Alzheimer's patients and others affected by the disease. Photo albums assist trained professionals in treating patients with the disease because the scrapbook format serves as a therapeutic restorative biography of the individual. A completed album can help people reconnect with their past."

Another reason scrapbooking has become more significant is because grandparents and parents can document and preserve both the ordinary and the extraordinary moments of their children's lives. There, in photographic and written form, is a history of celebrations, friendships, and family moments. Children gain a great deal of self-confidence when they see their accomplishments are important enough to be valued and preserved in a family or individual album. My grown children constantly review their albums and continue to add to them. What an incredible legacy to pass on.

As you can see, scrapbook albums have come a long way from yellowed newspaper articles and photos held in place by gummed corner pieces. The number one item people rescue from burning homes is their albums and pictures.

Themed Albums

Themed albums are all the rage. It seems the categories are endless. Numerous themes such as vacation, tribute (for a once-in-a-lifetime event), baby, wedding, birthday, heritage (to capture our ancestors and past), holiday, pets, promotions, hobbies, and more keep retailers hopping to stay on top of trends, new techniques, and merchandise arriving in their stores at warp speed.

Thirteen years ago my father passed away from prostate cancer. He left to me his treasured photograph albums, one of which was a carefully and lovingly created collection by his mother. In it were newspaper clippings of all his athletic achievements, his letters from home during his years away in Germany during World War II, and pictures of his status as a Marine, all carefully documented. The engagement announcement declaring the impending marriage of my mother and father was there along with a wedding napkin, photos, and testimonials from the best man and wedding attendants.

Another album is a genealogy of my family on my father's side with photos dating back to when my great-great-grandfather was a sheriff in Idaho. These mementos are indispensable to me, as they are to others lucky enough to have them.

Studies have shown that families are moving back to more traditional values. Women and men have carved their niche in the business world, examined the sexual revolution, and are experiencing the baby boomer aftermath. Tired and somewhat disillusioned by the drive to be bigger and better, they are now looking for down-home values that have been missing in the busy technological world around us. Enter the scrapbooking craze! We are no different from our ancestors. We all want to be remembered and have our lives validated; to pass on to our followers our beliefs, triumphs, tragedies, and everyday experiences and revelations in this thing we call Life. And frankly, that's where paste and scissors just don't cut it.

TODAY'S MARKETPLACE

"U.S. Craft and Hobby Industry Valued at $25.7 Billion," cried the headline of a recent article from the *HIA Nationwide Craft and Hobby Consumer Usage and Purchase Study*. The value of the craft and hobby industry in the United States grew to $25.7 billion in 2001, an 11 percent increase, compared to $23 billion in 2000, the caption declared.

It went on to say that HIA found that residents of 58 percent of U.S. households participated in crafts and hobbies in 2001, up from 54 percent in 2000. Findings also concluded that craft chains gained significant market share in 2001 in the sale of craft products.

As reported in the 2000 study, craft and hobby participants in 2001 were more likely to be married with children, more educated, and with a higher income than noncrafters. Women in these households tended to be younger and employed part-time. Heavy users, who made up 24 percent of the total participants in the survey, accounted for 69 percent of total dollar sales. *Selection* was this customer's primary reason for store choice.

The popularity of scrapbooking has burst from the faux-painted walls of today's homes, however. Hotels and spas are beginning to offer scrapbooking retreats as part of vacation packages. Traveling classes and weekend retreats are gathering enthusiasts from around the world. Websites such as *www.highcountryretreats.com, www.momandmescrapbooks.com,* and *www.getawaygals.com* are offering trips to those who can't seem to get enough of this scrapbooking phenomenon.

Scrapbooks probably sprang up during the Victorian era; that era's influence is still felt today. Pieces of treasured fabric and elaborately printed paper were saved and pressed into books. The art of decoupage was created during this era, and the frilly, often ostentatiously decorated cupids, Victorian fans, and ladies are still a popular seller in scrapbook stores. This is one market that draws from the old and cherished as well as the new and innovative.

In any given scrapbook, you can find everything from a child's overall button (carefully placed next to the picture of him wearing the outfit at the age of four) to embossed plaques, elaborate cutouts, ribbons, detailed craft paper, stickers, decals, brads, gel-penned entries, glow-in-the-dark emblems, scraps of material, hair, and party favors. And believe me, this list does not even scratch the surface. Walk into any scrapbook store and be prepared to be bowled over by the selection of merchandise. One can literally spend hundreds of dollars on the banquet of decoration and revolutionary preservative materials available.

One example is the lignin-free papers used for photo display. Lignin is a substance in paper that breaks down to become acidic over time. For anything of archival value, anything less than lignin-free is unheard of.

The word "buffered" is also being tossed about to describe the paper's ability to neutralize acids that could spread from one photo to another on a single sheet of paper.

If you enter the word "scrapbooking" in a search engine you will find over 39,000 Web sites. These sites include notices of conventions, expos, trade shows, classes in scrapbooking offered all over the world, Internet merchandise stores, consultants, importers, home-based businesses offering their services, and patented new inventions. This plethora of information and shopping convenience signifies the popularity of this new craze. Type in the store locator offered on many scrapbooking Web sites and a ribbon of store locations will unfurl like the periwinkle-blue streamer adorning the latest album.

With twenty million scrapbookers and 4,000 independent scrapbooking stores in the United States alone, the marketplace for this incredible hobby is flourishing.

According to *Creating Keepsakes Scrapbook Magazine* (*www. creatingkeepsakes.com*), Western states showed the most households involved in the hobby (between 23 and 26 percent of households), followed closely by New England states (20 percent of households). According to this same magazine, there are three core segments of scrapbookers: 1) the casual (novice), 2) the hobbyist (intermediate), and 3) the dedicated. Dedicated scrapbookers spend more than $50 a month on supplies, own $1,584 in merchandise, and spend more than ten hours a week scrapbooking.

Almost one half of hobbyists purchase or subscribe to craft/hobby related magazines and newsletters. Almost an equal number watch craft/hobby related television shows. The Home and Garden Television network (HGTV) has gained enormous popularity over the past few years. I have found the only drawback to these television programs is getting up from the chair and returning to daily activities, as the shows are presented back to back with unlimited decorating ideas. My family is seriously considering canceling my subscription to cable television.

The market and the dollars spent in the scrapbooking industry have yet to peak. More stores appear each year in the Yellow Pages, and home-based businesses thrive. These businesses allow many women a chance to use their latent creative talents and provide an income in one fell swoop. The advantages are heady and seduce new hopefuls each year.

SCRAPBOOKING CAREERS

It should be obvious by now that the scrapbooking industry has its doors wide open to those wishing to pursue a career in this field. The enthusiasm for scrapbooking is not unlike the popularity generated for faux painting a couple of years ago, when it hit the wallpaper industry over the head. The success of my book *How to Start a Faux Painting or Mural Business* attests to the numbers of creative men and women still flowing into this relatively new market. The emphasis on home and family has boded well for both the decorative painting market and now, scrapbooking.

The following careers are currently available in the scrapbooking arena:

1. The Home-Based Business

2. The Retail Store

3. The Internet Store

4. Teacher (both home and retail)

5. Scrapbook Consultant

6. Scrapbook Commissioned Albums

7. Designer (new products)

8. Event Planner

9. Freelance Writer

10. Importer

11. Freelance Artist

Each of these careers will be dealt with individually in the book with quotes and advice from professionals already making their mark in their chosen area. In the following chapter, The Skills of an Entrepreneur, we will go over the skills and knowledge needed to begin your own business. The specific skills relative to the chosen scrapbook career will be covered in the specific chapter on that career.

SOME INTERESTING STATISTICS

We have covered many statistics already for this creative industry. However, I have few more to tantalize you with:

- The breakdown of how people use their craft/hobby projects is: gifts (71%); home decorating (69%); personal use (62%); holiday decorating (59%); items to sell (16%).

- At present, the typical crafter/hobbyist spends an average of 7.5 hours per week engaged in his/her craft/hobby.

- The major sources from which craft/hobby participants get their ideas are magazines, books, and catalogs. Family and friends are also a good source.

- The scrapbooking industry is growing at a 25 percent rate.

- Magazine circulation increase is roughly 33 percent in the scrapbooking market, both domestically and internationally.

- People interested in careers in the scrapbooking industry are working either part-time or full-time, or starting new companies.

More and more products are being manufactured overseas, so the market for importers in this industry is growing, according to Michele Gerbrandt of *Memory Makers* magazine. The need for freelance artists for magazines, catalogs, and print work for television programming is also on the rise.

As the need for improved products—a "better mousetrap" of sorts—increases, the job opportunities in this rich market climb right along with it. Let's face it: When it comes to creativity, there is no ceiling unless you can put a cap on the human brain's capacity for imagination. The scrapbooking industry has unrolled the red carpet, welcoming all those with the ingenuity and passion to spring that new trap on a waiting and eager market. Now, let's see if having the right "cheese" is enough to begin a lucrative business.

CHAPTER 2

The Skills of the
Entrepreneur

The most successful business entrepreneurs are those who do what they enjoy. Period. End of sentence. Enthusiasm for your business is more important than the details of accounting, organization, etc. Why? Because you can always hire professionals to do the accounting, legal, and other work for your business and the cost won't be that great.

What you cannot buy is enthusiasm, drive, and know-how. Only *you* have these attributes for *your* business! The more you believe in your product or service and the benefits your customers derive from it, the more likely you are to succeed and prosper in your business. Only you can come up with an idea unique to your imagination, talent, and drive.

Wait! Stop! Before you order your shingle and put a nail above your door, there is the flip side. According to the Small Business Association (SBA), more than 50 percent of all new businesses in the United States fail. The main reason for these discouraging numbers is that many entrepreneurs get an idea for a business, very often based on a hobby they enjoy, and jump right in. The word "failed" may sound very frightening; remember, the SBA is only keeping track of whether a business remained open and viable. In many cases, it may be that when people attempted to turn their hobby into a profession, they discovered that they did not enjoy the business aspects, and closed by choice—it doesn't necessarily mean that they became financially destitute, or even that no one wanted to buy their services. For example, it might be that they found the hours were longer and more arduous than the job they quit to become their own boss. Perhaps they realized their work habits or personalities were not conducive to setting up shop. Be honest about your goals and reasons for going into business for yourself. It's not for everyone. You aren't playing with paper and scissors any longer. You have decided to go into business and create an income—serious stuff. Before coloring your logo and rushing off to the nearest graphic designer, you will need to ask yourself if you have what it takes.

DO YOU HAVE WHAT IT TAKES?

There are two categories in the area of business that you must address to determine whether you are entrepreneurial material: personal attributes and business acumen. Let's address the personal side of business first.

Personal Attributes

Let me ask you something to start with: Do you scrapbook yourself? Do you have a full-blown love (and hopefully passion) for creating one-of-a-kind albums, and are you knowledgeable about all the gadgets, papers, and terminology out there? If you are without a better-than-average grasp of what scrapbooking is all about and lack access to the latest trends and merchandise, why would anyone hire you or frequent your retail or Internet outlet? Sure, you can read books about it and interview scrapbook enthusiasts, but unless you've created albums yourself and know what makes a well-balanced page and how color coordination works and what devices create what effects, your customers will notice your lack of authentic expertise. Only by using the products and spending countless hours applying your imagination to a blank page will you be able to answer questions and recommend ideas and products with confidence. You can't learn creativity from a book.

Many home-based and retail scrapbook business owners confided that it was only after years of actually creating scrapbooks and experimenting with all the merchandise out there that they are now able to truthfully tell a customer which product did the best job and offer creative techniques the manufacturer had not even thought of. Would you let someone steam-clean your carpets who had just started a cleaning service, and who thought all he had to do was buy the equipment and put his logo on the side of a van? Or, would you choose a dedicated workman who had cleaned hundreds of carpets and knew the correct product to use for certain stains, thus eliminating any possible damage to your costly rugs or upholstery?

Now, what corner of the scrapbook enterprise do you want to occupy? Do you enjoy getting up in front of people and leading a group, or does the mere thought of that turn your hands clammy? Are you a team player, or a spectator who prefers her alone time?

Can you multitask and coordinate? Are you comfortable delegating, as you would have to with employees? How are you at bookkeeping, ordering, or being firm with vendors or unreasonable customers? Do you usually collapse under stressful situations or deadlines?

How are your customer service skills—do most people irritate you easily?

Can you work long hours at a retail site, or do you prefer sporadic spurts of energy at home, where you can do other things? Can you plan ahead, and can you manage your time? Are you an organized person, or does your bedroom closet look like Jack Dempsey just used your wardrobe for punching practice?

If you work at home, can you discipline your family and friends to respect your work hours and office space? Do you currently keep to a household budget and track expenses? Do you save for large purchases, or do you demand instant gratification? How would you handle loneliness if you worked long hours without others around you?

How about professionalism? You will be expected to present yourself well to bank personnel, vendors, advertising and marketing agents, commercial real estate agents (if you're going retail), maintenance personnel, landlords, and most of all, your customers. If you can't see yourself in anything other than Levis and sandals, you might want to rethink joining the professional field.

Are you a problem-solver who loves a challenge, or does facing one problem after another find you hiding under the covers? And finally, are you a risk-taker, or do you prefer to sail your boat closer to the shore?

Business Acumen

Now let's look at your business discernment. There are many traits you will need and skills you will have to acquire to run your own business. In chapter 12, under Contracts, Forms, and Checklists you will find a checklist of the qualifications we are about to discuss, so that you may check them off as you either implement them or gain the corresponding knowledge. Here is a rundown to consider:

You will have to decide what structure you want your business to run under (more about this in chapter 3). Do you want a partner? Are you planning to run a corporation, or will you be running a home-based business? You will need to register your business, deciding if it is service-oriented or if you will need a retail sales license. You will be creating a logo, business plan, tax foundation, letterhead, invoices, inventory control sheets, and vendor base. Whether your office is home-based or not, you will need to acquire office equipment and, if you go into retail, a profusion of displays, merchandise, and tracking equipment. The ability to advertise and attract customers will be crucial. Can you evaluate the competition and offer something it does not? How are your computer skills? Will you be creating a Web site? Do you know how to handle today's necessary technology? Do you know how to price inventory and monitor its progress?

You see? There is so much more to running a business than deciding it would be fun to be your own boss and sell pretty stickers to happy scrappers. Without the business backbone needed to start and operate a business, you could fall flat on your paste.

FIGURING OUT WHERE YOU FIT IN

Try this quick feedback question to establish where you think you fit in:

The scrapbooking business area that would be the most attractive to me is:

_____

because I have the following skills and interests to bring to the business to make it a success: _____

_____.

In the first blank, choose the facet of scrapbooking you are drawn to at the moment, i.e., consultant, home-based business, retail owner, Internet store owner, teacher, etc. In the second blank, list all the assets you feel you have that would enable you to be a success at that particular scrapbook career. Now you have at least an idea of where you feel you want to go and what strengths and weaknesses you have for that chosen area.

To help you further facilitate your decision to go into business, let's break it down even more.

Would you like to work with people? A "people business" is one where you work day in and day out with—you guessed it—people. You must enjoy your customers, or they will sense it and possibly take their business elsewhere. If you can't present a polished, professional, friendly manner consistently, then go into a "loner" area of this business.

A typical scrapbooking career for you "people-friendly" folk would be to open a retail outlet and actually work the store yourself. Another avenue would be to become a consultant who helps people or stores acquire their dreams in the scrapbooking circuit. A teacher who runs workshops and seminars would do well here. One whose heart is in the trade show side of things might also flourish.

What if you prefer working alone with minimal contact with "homosapiens"—yes—people! You would then feel more at home designing your own products in your studio and shopping them around to manufacturers via a Web site or mail. Someone who creates commissioned albums would do most of the work from home, as would a freelance artist for the expanding scrapbook magazine market. Under chapter 6, The Electric Entrepreneur, you'll discover all you need to know about starting your own Internet business, which is primarily done behind the scenes.

There is no part of any business that is completely people-free, as you will be dealing with vendors, bankers, and customers on some level. But you can select the area that fits inside your comfort zone for interaction. You can decide if you want a stay-at-home business, or one run outside the home, with only minimal details handled in a home office.

TEN FEARS THAT BLOCK SUCCESS

There is a reason why many people feel happier working for an employer, besides the obvious relief of letting someone else deal with tax hassles, lay-offs, overhead, and employee issues. The thought of opening a business where you are the boss and fingers point toward you, whether in times of loss or profit, can be a pretty scary scenario. For this reason, I have listed the ten most common fears people have voiced when deciding whether or not to go into business for themselves.

1. The overall fear of failure, where one is surrounded by a general sense of dread and anxiety.

2. Fear of success: Will I be overwhelmed and my life no longer my own?

3. Fear of embarrassment if it should fail.

4. Fear of demands on time.

5. Fear of being undereducated for the job requirements.

6. Fear of being your own boss: "The buck stops here!"

7. Fear of competition.

8. Fear of all the details: accounting, legalities, setting up a Web site, health insurance, retirement protection, etc.

9. Fear of depleted family time.

10. Fear of customer dissatisfaction.

If any or a few of these fears are nibbling at your mind, I have good news for you—you're normal! There is not one of us opening a business for the first time or the fifteenth time who does not have these little cuties as bed partners every night. "What if?" becomes our new mantra, until our friends and families are ordering Valium. Fears are like packed earth to a worm—you just keep wiggling and working through them. You eventually get there and may have the good luck of leaving a tunnel you've blazed for others to "worm through" as well. One of my favorite quotes is, "Fear knocked at the door; courage answered and no one was there."

I'd like to mention something you may not have thought about. By looking fear in the face and taking a risk, you provide an example to your children, friends, and family, who are watching you and assessing your results. A child raised around a parent or significant role model will learn that she too can go after her dreams.

I was raised in a modeling agency my mother created out of our home. At the age of five, I was on a runway, and the confidence and people skills that experience gave me are immeasurable. But it was the day in, day out of watching her overcome every obstacle and compete with the franchised modeling agencies and come out on top that put the foundation under my feet and the clouds in my hands. "You can be anything you want to, Becky," was served up daily with breakfast. How can you hand your child a better tool for the future (with the exception of good foundational beliefs and perspective)?

The reason fear sinks so many would-be entrepreneurs is the fact that it represents the unknown—that spooky Never Never Land that waits for us somewhere "out there." You have it a little better than those who have been the absolute first to create a market, however. Others have gone before you and proven the area was "monster-free." They have even kindly handed you a flashlight in the guise of shared expertise and advice, and unrolled maps showing you where the pitfalls are and how to avoid them. Not so bad, really. So pick up your machete and compass, put on a brave face, and go boldly out into this wonderful adventure called entrepreneurship. I've been traveling its paths for over twenty-five years, and you couldn't get me to hand in my road map for any amount of money.

QUICK LIST METHOD TO SET YOUR GOALS

Most people I've been around who wanted to start their own business didn't for a number of reasons. The one I found that frustrated me the most was laziness. When they took a look at all it required to even get started, they balked, pouted . . . and quit. There are guaranteed failures out there: the ones who never start.

I read somewhere about a woman who was in her sixties and told her husband she had always wanted to go back to school and become a certified psychologist. He encouraged her to do it now. With incredulous eyes, she stared at him and burst out, "I will be seventy-two by the time I open my practice!"

"Well," said her husband mildly, "you're going to be seventy-two anyway. Do you want to be seventy-two and living your dream as a psychologist, or just seventy-two and still wishing you had followed your heart?"

That man deserves some major brownies!

So, my fellow entrepreneurs, let's eliminate the laziness factor right now. I will show you, step by step, how to get off your hand-stitched cushion and begin to follow your heart today.

First Things First

Decide which area(s) of the scrapbooking field you want to go into: consulting, store owner, teacher, etc. That's the first thing. You need to know the destination in order to plan a road map.

Now, will you be working from your home, or leasing space somewhere? This answer will determine many things, such as capital needed to open your business, zoning regulations if you're working from home, the need for employees, etc. Decide now, based on what you've already read here, which scrapbooking avenue you prefer, so that you can determine whether it is suitable for the home, or if you need bigger digs. All of these things will be covered in detail in their respective chapters, but my goal here is to get you seated comfortably in a chair with pen and paper and actually generate some action.

Alright, you've made two decisions already: 1) Which scrapbooking career makes your heart go pitter-pat, and 2) Whether the invoice will have your home address on it or an outside business location.

I would like to mention at this juncture that the precursor to a decision to run a home-based business should be a family meeting to determine how much support you may expect. This will be highlighted in chapter 4, The Home-Based Scrapbooking Business, but for now, I would encourage you to invite all proponents and opponents to voice their thoughts.

Next on our quick list is determining funding. Will you be pulling monies to begin this business from a savings account, anticipating rich Uncle Harry's demise, or is a loan indicated? If a loan will be necessary, how's your credit? Will there be a partner to share start-up costs? Should you start this venture part-time until more money is available to go full out?

Now find a place by your favorite phone, pop a soda, and secure some quiet time. You are about to become very well acquainted with your telephone keypad and your handy Yellow Pages.

Your first stop will be to call your state revenue department to inquire about registering your business. Details of registering are in the following chapter. All I want you to do right now is make a few calls that will enable you to see that all things that seem overwhelming at first are easily broken down into doable steps. Making a few phone calls will show you this.

Your next call will be to your insurance agent; if you don't have one, now is the time to find one. Ask what insurances you would have to carry for your type of business and specify whether it will be home-based or retail. Jot all the information down. It's highly likely that any of these calls will send you out on other calls, but that's great! You're gathering information and feeling empowered.

If you are hanging your shingle above your own front door, you will need to call the zoning commission with the Planning and Development Department of your county.

If you are feeling really bold, call a commercial realty agent and ask questions about possible retail sites available in the area of town in which you think your business would thrive. Location really is key, and the agent will have suggestions for the best venues based on your type of business. This one phone call will give you an insight into what we will cover in chapter 5, Going Retail.

I don't want you to head into the murkier waters of taxes, structures, bank accounts, and bookkeeping right now. My purpose here is to get your feet wet in the shallow end and hand you the tools to begin. Everything you need for your area of business will be covered *thoroughly* in the following chapters. What I've found, however, is that many take a look at those chapter subheads and feel their shoulders slump. Taking a little time *today* to make a few calls and jot down a handful of decisions will prove to you that it is not so scary and can be accomplished *one step at a time*.

I learned to break down seemingly insurmountable tasks while making a career as a muralist. Staring at a thirty-five-foot wall or a fifty-foot semi-trailer truck and knowing I had to fill every inch of that space with creative images was daunting, believe me! The only way I handled it was to take a deep breath and say, "Okay Becky, you don't have to paint the entire thing today. Concentrate on this one area here (and I would block out a doable space for the day), and that's all you have to do today. Nothing else—just this one area." So each day, I would show up, paint my designated area, step back, and feel good about what I had accomplished, and go home. Before I knew it, the mural was completed.

There are times I see my work around town in Fort Collins, Colorado, on some of the major projects and wonder how I found the courage to start that wall. It's like what someone said about eating: If you had to look at a gigantic table spread with all the food you would be eating in your lifetime, wouldn't you feel overwhelmed and shout, "Good grief . . . you expect me to eat all *that?*" Well, silly, you don't eat it all *now*! Just a day at a time, and enjoy the sensation.

If you are feeling better and have decided you really do want to start your own business, then do some fun things associated with it. Doodle some ideas for your logo. Look through the Yellow Pages of several surrounding cities and see what types of ads others in your chosen field have put together, and what benefits their businesses offer. You may see a few you hadn't thought of. Collect magazines (if you haven't already) on the scrapbooking industry and study them thoroughly. Inside is a wealth of information on not only new industry trends, but also ideas of what customers are looking for.

Do you have a few goals set now? You should; small ones that turn into completed projects. Please don't skip this important part. If you tend to procrastinate or become overwhelmed with minutiae, just make a few calls and you'll feel energized, I promise.

LET'S SEE WHAT'S IN YOUR FUTURE

You have a good idea and you've researched the market and found it favorable for profit-producing potential (PPP). This idea does not have to be totally original, just a good match for the market.

Russ Williams of Invention Home, an incredible Web site for new inventors and their creative ideas, *www.inventionhome.com*, told me that an invention does not have to be an original idea, simply a needed modification or improvement of an existing idea that has created a popular demand in a given market.

If you have an idea for new areas of consulting that have not been tapped, or a variance on an existing technique which you believe would increase sales, then your future could be very profitable indeed.

Maybe you have more than just an idea; you have a marketable skill. You are adept at creating new themes and page décor using existing merchandise, or coming up with your own artistic creations.

Now analyze the scrapbooking market and determine what you can and want to do and find your niche. If that niche is in the custom-colored walls of your own home, you still have much to do. Creating the atmosphere and space for a home-based business has its challenges, and you must weather the legalities of running a business from home as well.

The retail and Internet businesses are replete with regulations, red tape, and financing configurations. Am I telling you this to frighten you off? Of course not. I merely want to inform you that your future is dependent on your ability to deal with business matters in a professional way.

One complaint I do hear from people who have turned a beloved hobby into a business is that what was once a fun, creative release is now work! Try very hard to keep the passion you originally felt for scrapbooking and infuse your new business with that enthusiasm. It is not uncommon for someone skilled in a particular area to have people seek out their abilities; this suddenly becomes, "Wow . . . I could make a living at this!" Once the doors are open and the cash register is ringing and the bills are due and complaints are logged, that little hobby you used to adore is now a job with overhead and demands.

Find a way in the beginning to anticipate these common hindrances to a business and maintain that devotion you feel for what got you here. I constantly remind myself that not only do I get to do what I love, but it provides me an income as well. Keep it in perspective and know all endeavors have their annoyances, and that's all they are—routine annoyances.

If you have the knowledge, skill, and passion to become a business owner in this incredible, explosive field, there is nothing stopping you. With this book as a guide and a strong belief in yourself, I foresee great things in that crystal ball before you. Wipe the glue and paste smudges off its shiny surface and go after your scrapbooking dreams!

CHAPTER 3

Setting Up Shop

"Nothing is more powerful than an idea whose time has come."

Victor Hugo wrote that, and its message inspires me daily. Now it's your turn to take that dream of yours and turn it into a viable business.

LEGAL STRUCTURE

Your new venture will need to be set up as a legal structure. Your business will be created under one of these basic forms: a sole proprietorship, a partnership, or a corporation. Please consider carefully your needs and financial backing before you select the structure you want to register your company with. Most home-based businesses are sole proprietorships, but partnerships are not unheard of; full-out corporations are a little rarer. Your structural decision will impact many areas of your business, including how your taxes are filed. Partnerships and corporations will require contracts and legal fees, negotiations between the parties, and a division of responsibility.

There are numerous Web sites and books with information on starting a business and on which structure will work for your particular setup. By typing the keywords "small business" in your Web browser, you will find numerous sites to help you make this vital decision. One Web site that many of my friends have used is Nolo Press, at *www.nolopress.com*. Download *Choosing a Structure for Your Small Business*. There is a $10 charge, which buys you a wealth of information.

The Small Business Start-up Guide by Robert Sullivan is an excellent book for newbies in the work force. One of the many popular "Idiot" series books is *The Complete Idiot's Guide to Starting Your Own Business* by Ed Paulson, which I highly recommend.

Let's take a look at these three structural choices: sole proprietor, partnership, or corporation.

SOLE PROPRIETOR

Most small businesses choose this form in part because it is the easiest and least expensive. It's a good way to get your feet wet and grow your company before you decide to take on a partner or fly your flag under a corporate logo. You are the only owner, and from a legal viewpoint and tax perspective there is no differentiation between you and the business. You will make all the decisions, bank all the profits, and accept all the congratulations.

On the flip side, you will incur all the debt, handle disgruntled customers, and dodge the "I-told-you-so's" if and when your venture fails. All your personal assets are on the line if the business fails, and creditors can attack your home, car, and large investments if it goes to court. If you used your home as collateral for a business loan, it's on the line.

As a sole proprietor, you may hire employees to work for you, which could involve taking on workman's compensation and unemployment insurance. You may need to provide vehicle coverage for employees as well if they are using their car for business purposes, such as deliveries, pickup, etc.

I have always been a sole proprietor and have never had any problems. Yes, health insurance is expensive when you are flying solo, and you will need to get permits and licenses, but these are trivial compared to the regulations that exist for forming a partnership or corporation. I wanted the autonomy of being my own boss and setting things up the way I want them. I like having things orderly, and actually enjoyed the process of setting up my own shop and knowing I had crossed all the *t*s and dotted all the *i*s.

I've outsourced work to other freelance artists before and found myself frustrated. Suddenly, the control I had over my business and what happened in "my name" was gone; the results were now in someone else's hands. Many times, I received calls from a dissatisfied client, and I would have to make things right and take time away from my projects to correct the problem. What started out as a means to relieve myself from some of the pressure turned out to be more work.

The times that I've worked with another artist, however, did have their plus sides. There was someone to talk to, joke with, brainstorm with, and share expenses and workload with. But in the long run, I knew it would take a toll, as I have a certain way of doing things. Often you will find when working with someone else that your timetables don't match. You may be someone who rises with the rooster and your partner may rise with the noon school bell. You're organized—she prefers the "lived-in" look. You dress for meetings, while her attire can only be described as "casually ruffled."

Of course, as a sole proprietor, you can have employees, but at least in the beginning, you'll probably run the whole show yourself—until you get a firm grip on the ropes involved in running a new business. As a sole owner, you will answer the phones, file the invoices, pay the bills, handle the advertising and complaints, haggle over back orders of merchandise, attend business meetings alone, negotiate insurance, and smile for the customer.

You can also take a break when you feel like it, not when someone else is ready. You decide your work hours and how your business will be run, along with what customer service policy you believe is effective. Negotiation hassles are nonexistent, and there isn't that uncomfortable feeling that you are doing more work than your partner.

To be honest, the biggest perk of working alone is the peace of mind it brings me over the fact that there is nothing "out there" not being taken care of. You can delegate responsibilities to someone else, but you always have to follow up (or you should). When my to-do list is checked off at the end of the day, I feel relaxed knowing things are in control and there are no loose ends dangling. But, that's my personality. You may be different and require a partner to hold the template while you fill in the lines.

PARTNERSHIP

Just because a friend shares your enthusiasm for scrapbooking does not necessarily make her a good business partner choice. There are extremely important considerations when deciding who will share responsibility in your profit-producing enterprise.

The most important consideration is financial. If you have a partner, you and she will share the financial burden of the business. You will both be accountable for supporting the business during hard times, and paying the IRS at tax times. The other considerations have to do with how well your personalities and styles complement each other. How would your personalities get along during long work hours? Do you thrive on challenges and obstacles while your friend tends to buckle? Is one of you a "people" person, or do you both tend to be shy and avoid confrontations? If you are terrific with numbers and bookkeeping and your new partner thrives on interacting with customers, then it's a good match. However, if neither of you has any business acumen when it comes to numbers and your exploding garage is an indication of your organizational skills, then reconsider your pairing. Being able to rattle off the names of the top sticker manufacturers is not enough to set up shop.

If you've found the perfect partner and you are both scribbling names for the new business on napkins and leftover paper borders, then great. Now, sit down and ask the tough questions:

- What do both of you see as your mission statement? What goals do you have for the business?

- Who will invest what?

- Which responsibilities will each of you have? Write them down. Purchasing? Bookkeeping? Marketing?

- Will one of you be the primary decision-maker, or will everything require a "huddle"?

- How and when will profits be divided?

- How will you buy each other out in the future?

- How will vacation time be divided up? Who works what hours?

This is not a time to worry about treading on someone's feelings. These things must be hammered out ahead of time, and it will give you a good indication of just how compatible you and your partner are. If the new business buddy happens to be your spouse, take a good hard look at how you handle the family finances and long periods of time together. Many marriages have ended up in boxing arenas when they chiseled LLC next to

Mr. and Mrs. (An LLC encompasses aspects of both a partnership and a corporation—I'll explain below.)

Sit down with a lawyer and have a contract drawn up! Do *not* settle for a piece of lined legal paper with your two names dutifully jotted at the bottom and a date as the only record of your business expectations and liabilities. That sweet face exploding with enthusiasm for your new venture could turn into the biggest frown you've ever seen when things founder or the newness wears off. Get it in writing! Cover your bases and know that if things don't work out the way you had hoped, the legal system can straighten it out.

A partnership still has unlimited liability, and each partner could be held liable for all the debts the business accrues. You could lose your assets based on a bad decision your partner made.

You might create a limited partnership where one partner (the general partner) has unlimited liability, while the limited partner is only liable for as much as she has invested in the business, much like an investor, while the general partner runs the business.

My biggest piece of advice when considering a partner is equal division of workload and responsibility—unless your partner is coming onboard as an investor only. Nothing sours a relationship faster than one person doing all the worrying, work, and upkeep. How are your family responsibilities? If one of you has five small children and the other is an empty-nester, odds are the nest-free person will carry more of a workload. Once you've heard "I have to take Little Elmer to swimming practice" for the ninth time, you may feel the niggling irritation of a one-sided work shift. And please remember, when dealing with family members, it gets tricky. Favors are suddenly cashed in, and because you are good old Uncle Ralph, surely you can cover for Cousin Ray while he takes up his buddy's offer on that once-in-a-lifetime fishing trip to Montana. In short, know who you are forming a business marriage with. Forget the manners and hit the tough questions *now*!

CORPORATION

A corporation is a legal entity. It protects you from lawsuits against your personal assets. If you're considering opening a retail store, a corporation would be a good choice. Other high-voltage careers such as event planner, importer, or product designer would also benefit from this structural umbrella.

Forming a corporation is more complex and requires an attorney, and it does require maintenance. There are contracts and legal fees. Corporations are taxed on their own income, and the company shareholders pay tax again on their salaries and dividends. You form a Board of Directors and file reports. In short, you are running a professional business, and there will be legal repercussions if the "articles" are not adhered to.

S Corporations

If you've decided to run a home-based business, an S Corporation might be desirable. This structure is geared toward small businesses, and an S Corp does not pay taxes on its income. Income and expenses are divided among shareholders, who report them on their income tax returns. The liability in an S Corp is limited; however, there are reporting standards and heavy bookkeeping requirements. It does offer the small business owner some wonderful coverage and options, but it may be something you could grow into if not needed for your initial growth period. Most small businesses do not need shareholders, directors, and the hassles of keeping meeting minutes and corporate records.

Limited Liability Companies

Limited Liability Companies, or LLCs, are the new kids on the block, and they're receiving lots of playtime offers. Since LLCs avoid double taxation and still offer limited liability, they have many business owners touting their benefits.

Each state has its own LLC regulations that you must adhere to. Check with your state department of revenue, or look up some Web sites dealing with LLCs. The one I found the most informative and thorough is Business Filings Incorporated, at *www.bizfilings.com*.

An LLC will require you to set up Articles of Organization and file them with the state, along with filing fees, initial franchise taxes, and other fees. As a legal requirement, you do not need an attorney to file the Articles of Organization, but make sure you understand the requirements set forth by your particular state.

Choose the name of your LLC carefully, says Business Filings Incorporated. It is very important that your name portray the image you want for your new company. Legally, the name you select must not be "deceptively similar" to any existing company, and it must be "distinguishable on the record" for your state.

For example, if an LLC named Flower LLC exists in your state, you probably would not be allowed to name your business Flour Limited Liability Company. You should always have a follow-up name in case the one you want is taken. Most states require that you show your business is a limited liability company by using the acronym LLC, or the actual words, as part of your business name.

The IRS does allow one member LLCs to qualify for pass-through tax treatment; however, taxation of one-person LLCs at the state level may be different.

LLC or S Corporation?

While the S Corporation's special tax status eliminates double taxation, it lacks the flexibility of an LLC in allocating income to the owners, according to Business Filings Incorporated. An LLC may offer several classes of membership interests while an S corporation may have one class of stock. Any number of individuals or entities may own interests in an LLC. However, ownership interest in an S corporation is limited to no more than seventy-five shareholders, who must be individuals (either U.S. citizens or permanent resident aliens). Also, S corporations cannot be owned by C corporations, other S corporations, many trusts, LLC partnerships, or nonresident aliens. LLCs are allowed to own subsidiaries without restriction.

To learn more about the similarities and differences between S corporations and LLCs, go to *www.bizfilings.com*. For advice regarding which entity is best for your particular situation, it would be best to consult an attorney or accountant.

REGISTERING

If you will be operating as a sole proprietor or general partnership, you must register your business trade name with the Department of Revenue in your state. You can contact your Chamber of Commerce or Small Business Development for further information based on your state's regulations.

Once you've created a name for your business, simply go your Department of Revenue or appropriate federal office and register it. The form is simple, usually a page, and the fee is nominal—as little as $8 in some states. It takes about thirty minutes, and you become an official business owner.

Typically there will be a search for a similar name, so always have a second name in the bullpen just in case the one you've selected has been taken. Even after you've registered your trade name, it is possible another business in a different state or industry will register for the same name. Having yours registered will give you some protection in the case of a competitor trying to use your name.

Ask when you register if there is a time period to renew your trade name. It may lapse after a period of years and be up for grabs.

In Colorado, if you need to search for trade names for a corporation, limited liability company, limited liability partnership, or limited liability limited partnership, you must contact the Colorado Secretary of State. You will have to check with your state Department of Revenue to find out whom you need to contact.

Registration of a Trade Name with the Department of Revenue does not guarantee exclusive rights to that name. You will require an attorney to register your trademark with the U.S. Office of Patent and Trademark Registry. A trademark would be a good idea for any business you may run internationally, such as a Web site or store. Consult an attorney specializing in intellectual property law.

Before you register your name, read the section in this chapter called "It's All in the Name!" carefully. The selection of a name involves more than just a cute play on words or honoring your family lineage by naming the business with the family name.

INSURANCE

You will need business insurance for your new venture. If you are operating out of your home, your homeowner's policy may include all the coverage you require, but it is likely you will have to purchase business owner's insurance. If you're offering *crops* (meetings where people gather to work on their projects together) and workshops from your home, you may need additional liability insurance in case of an injury to a customer. Check with your insurance agent and make sure you are explicit about all of the activities you will be offering, including outdoor parking.

Like a comprehensive homeowner's policy, a business owner's policy protects against economic losses caused by damage to the owner's property and against legal liability for others for bodily injury and property damage involving the business.

Business Owner's Policy

A business owner's policy covers the same kind of protection from perils that the typical homeowner's policy does, but it does so for the business property.

Damage to Business Owner's Property

Example: A large tree limb falls on your home, wrecking a portion of your roof and the rooms below (cost to repair = $30,000) and damaging a personal computer system that was exclusively used in your home business (cost to repair = $2,000).

In this example, if you had only a homeowner's policy, you would either get only $30,000 (for the wrecked rooms and roof), or nothing at all, if your policy voided coverage if a business is conducted in the house. The full $32,000 worth of costs would be covered if you had a business coverage rider to your homeowner's policy, or if you had both a homeowner's and a business owner's policy.

In addition to this coverage, you can receive coverage, at extra cost, for income loss as a result of the business's property damage. A sprinkler system going off in a scrapbooking retail store could ruin the specialty papers and other merchandise, resulting in a loss of business.

Bodily Injury and Property Damage Liability

This is probably the most important part of the business owner's policy— certainly so if you have business visitors in your home. It will cover injuries to your customers, whether they were injured in the "personal" or in the "business" portion of your home.

Another type of coverage that you can add to a business owner's policy for extra protection is for product liability. If your business includes the selling of a product, you may be sued if someone is injured using the product. This can happen even if you just distributed the product, and had nothing to do with its design or manufacture. Depending on how potentially dangerous the product is, who the user will be, and in what part of the country it will likely be sold or used, the cost for this additional coverage could be reasonable or extremely expensive.

If you are planning to take part in a trade show or expo or any event on an outside property, check to see what liability insurance is carried by that particular venue and what, if any, additional coverage you may need to acquire.

Automobile Insurance

If you use your car in connection with your business, it's important that you find out if your policy will cover business-related accidents. Consider the devastating effect that a large judgment could have on your personal and business finances; you don't want to find out after the fact that you weren't covered. If your policy does not cover business travel, you usually can get coverage by way of a policy rider for a reasonable amount.

If you have employees who drive your car on business, you should have what is known as "non-owned" coverage. This coverage pays for injury to people and property damage caused by the employee.

IT'S ALL IN THE NAME!

Naming your business is important stuff. Your name, your dba (doing business as), will decide a lot of things for you now and down the road.

The temptation here is to go for clever and cutesy. If you can think of a clever name that clearly describes the product you are selling, that's great! If, however, it isn't clear exactly what you do offer, then you have a problem.

For example, a company called CreamIt: is it a cream pie business, cosmetics, a pie-throwing party service, or a dairy? Answer: a dairy. By all means be clever—people remember clever logos and names—but make sure it's immediately apparent what your business is offering.

If you are considering putting your name on the business, such as Wendy's Memory Savers, that's fine. It denotes a smaller, friendly shop with the owner's full attention. Lawyers and accountants often use their names as they are cashing in on their reputations and (hopefully) good name in the industry. There is one hitch to using your name, however. If you were to decide to sell the business later and it is closely tied to you, the new buyer may be hesitant. Is Wendy's still Wendy's without Wendy? Can you sell your customer base if you're out of the picture? What about handing the business down to your children? Will they want it to remain Wendy's, or want to change it to Memory Savers, Dude? Having your name instead of a generic one may also make it easier for your business to be accessible to legal attachments, such as personal liens or tax problems, which is a decidedly negative aspect. Think it over carefully.

Another thing to consider when choosing a name is the impression it gives. Do you want fun and playful or sophisticated and sharp? Pictures, Paste, and Press-ons is a cute scrapbook business name; it could go either way. Polly's Purty Pictures is obviously tongue-in-cheek and cutesy. Preserving Perfect Posterity creates an image of class and nostalgia.

When creating a logo, the name is very important in how it will translate in print and graphic images. The name may be so lengthy that is cumbersome on a letterhead, store sign, or vehicle lettering. If you're using a graphic, could the person looking at it tell what your business is without the name next to it?

A word of caution: If someone else has the name you've been dreaming of for eight months, don't try to hang on to it by altering it slightly. In the long run, it will only add to confusion with customers and animosity from the original owner. Be original—you're in a creative field!

SETTING UP YOUR BANK ACCOUNT

You will need to decide whether you will be separating your business banking from your personal banking (which I highly recommend). Many small-time home-based businesses simply keep their personal checking and add the letters DBA (Doing Business As) and their new business name after their personal name on their checks. This way, the checking account acts as a commercial account without obtaining two separate entities. The downside to this is the obvious: Keeping your personal expenditures separate from your business transactions is tricky, and many banks, when looking over your records, will frown on having to separate the two in order to make a loan decision. The IRS will also have a hard time deciding if this is a viable business or a hobby.

For the sake of accurate bookkeeping, open a separate business account. It is very important for corporations and LLCs to keep the finances of the business separate from those of the owners. To open a business bank account, most banks require information on the company, such as formation date and type of business, and names and addresses of its owners. Some banks require corporations to provide a resolution from the board of directors or members/managers authorizing the opening of the business bank account.

Your bank will need to see your registration form and a resale permit (more about permits in this chapter) in order to open your account and print up your checks—another reason for doing a trade name search. You wouldn't want to put your business name on your checks and find out when you go to register that the name has been taken.

RECORD-KEEPING

Good record-keeping is a must for any business. Whether you do the books with a store-bought ledger, use a computer spreadsheet, or hand over everything to an accountant, you must maintain accurate, daily records. Outside entities such as the IRS and bank loan officers will want to see your profit and loss statement (also called P & L) and monthly ledgers. Complete record-keeping charts are located in chapter 12: Contracts, Forms, and Checklists.

If you're comfortable with a computer and spreadsheet software, small business accounting packages such as QuickBooks or Peachtree Accounting make it a snap to do your bookkeeping. There is also tax preparation software (don't you just love computer technology?) to allow you to handle all your tax accounting needs. Another boon to computerized bookkeeping is the ability to do your books, download the information to a disk, and take it to your accountant for professional monthly, quarterly, and annual statements.

Resist the "throw the receipts in a shoebox and do it later" mindset. You won't remember everything, and once it all piles up, it can be overwhelming. Set aside a time at the end of each day to update daily transactions. You will be paying Uncle Sam quarterly anyway, so save yourself some aspirin and do your books regularly. The one-write system, in which you make account entries as part of your check writing, is a popular form of accounting for small businesses.

If your structure is a corporation or you have employees, an accountant would be a good idea. Spend your time bringing in revenue, not researching forms and tax breaks, when you get into this area.

Record-Keeping Terms

Whether you do your own books or hire an accountant, you will need to decide your *business year*. For most small businesses, the business year is the same as the calendar year, January 1 through December 31. This simplifies your taxes as a sole proprietor, as you'll be paying taxes based on a calendar year anyway.

The other type of accounting ruler would be a *fiscal year*. The fiscal year may begin any time at any month and end the previous day of the following year—for example, April 15, 2004, through April 14, 2005.

Two methods of accounting are the *cash method*, where income is dictated by when the check arrives and expenses are recorded when paid, and the *accrual method*. The accrual method, mainly used when inventory is involved, is based on income being recorded when an invoice is sent out and expenses recorded when the bill arrives. *Receivables* are money owed to you but not yet received, and *payables* are money you owe others but have not yet paid. These are listed as assets and liabilities on your monthly balance sheets; *www.bizfilings.com* has extensive information in this area.

A *profit and loss statement* (or *P & L*) gives an overview of your income and expenses over a given accounting period. The nice thing about a P & L is that it lets you see at a glance how your business is faring. It will not only give you a month's-end, bird's-eye view, but the year-to-date as well. The year-to-date shows you at a glance you are making a profit, what your expenses are running, and other pertinent figures for your business for that running year.

A *cash flow statement* is basically a comparison of money coming in and money going out. You can take a look at your projected cash flow and see if your business is on track or in trouble with upcoming bills.

And finally, a *balance sheet* lays out in black and white your businesses assets and liabilities. This report will show you, and anyone you may be approaching for a loan, exactly what your business is worth.

These methods of tracking your business's day-to-day activity are vital. They will tell you now if you are on target with what you projected your income and outflow to be; whether you are paying too much for inventory or have too much inventory and are not pricing it effectively; and whether you have a problem that needs to be addressed now! Sample ledgers and spreadsheets are found in chapter 12.

Save receipts, check stubs, and deposit slips even after you've recorded them. They are important as backup for the IRS or a possible return of merchandise. Accurate records of car mileage, gas, oil, and car maintenance are all important come tax time. These are used as deductions, and the depreciation of the vehicle can be determined as well.

If you use the same phone line for your home and business, keep a phone log.

Have a petty cash log available for small cash purchases pertaining to your business.

Travel expenses, including lodging, food, and transportation, should be jotted down. A log of fixed assets such as cars, office equipment, cameras, etc., will all need to be documented to determine depreciation. The importance of maintaining accurate inventory records should be self-evident.

If you're a retailer with daily receipts, you should clear the cash register daily and keep track of taxable sales in order to pay sales tax based on city and state regulations. Make your deposits daily or weekly so that revenue does not sit around.

Now, on a monthly basis, record your revenue accrued and expenses, and create a profit and loss statement. Balance your checkbook and update your cash flow projections and balance sheet.

If all this sounds daunting, then by all means, use an accountant or computerized accounting system. You enter each transaction one time, and the software will automatically create individual logs and records.

Point-of-Sale System (POS)

One final word on bookkeeping is a *point-of-sale (POS) system*. This is an automated method to manage inventory by tracking your product supply and feeding it into your cash register. This system is truly amazing. All your inventory purchases are entered based on a database. When you make a sale, it decreases the inventory account, and when you make a merchandise purchase, it increases it. You are notified of depleted merchandise and that it's time to order. At a glance, you can also see what's not moving and may need to hit the clearance bin.

"Check that a local manufacturer is bar-coded for your POS system," states Penny McDaniel of Legacies LLC, a successful Loveland scrapbooking store. "Look for a POS system tailored to scrapbooking stores."

Microsoft has a comprehensive system called the Microsoft Business Solutions Retail Management System. It is a POS solution designed primarily to meet the needs of medium-sized retailers. The product includes a customer tracking solution, provides inventory management tools, and has comprehensive reporting tools, among other features. Check out Microsoft's Web site at *www.microsoft.com/BusinessSolutions/Retail/Retail%20Management/Modules/retail_hq_overview.mspx*.

Other Web sites for POS systems are *www.SystemID.com*, an inventory management program, and Asset Management at *www.made2mange.com*.

LICENSES AND PERMITS

According to Business Filings Incorporated, most state and local governments require businesses operating in their area to obtain licenses or permits. In some instances, the federal government may also require you to obtain a license or permit.

Licenses

There are two types of licenses: general and specific. A general business license, similar to a use tax, is assessed annually for the privilege of operating a business in the jurisdiction. A special license is one that is issued to a business that will provide products or services that require regulation. Special licenses are issued to professionals such as doctors, lawyers, barbers, and others who have met a certain level of training or education.

A sales tax license is a must. According to Penny McDaniel, owner of Legacies LLC, "No one would work with me without a tax ID number; not wholesalers, catalogues—no one. It was difficult to research start-up costs without a tax ID. Product manufacturers wouldn't work with me. Trade shows and select vendors also wanted proof that I was a serious businessperson. Some manufacturers wanted to see a picture of the store and a copy of a lease agreement."

Check with your state or government office to see which licenses and permits are required for your business. Ask them for forms and information that your type of business may require. Your property may be subject to an inspection before a license or permit is granted.

Permits

Your home-based business may require a *zoning permit*. Zoning ordinances, which regulate how property can be used, are a common type of ordinance. If you comply with this ordinance, a permit will be granted for you to operate your business. For more about zoning see the "Laws Zoning" section of chapter 4, The Home-Based Scrapbooking Business.

Another important permit is a *resale permit*. If your state collects sales tax, you'll need one of these and can acquire one at your Department of Revenue. You must have it to do business. This permit will also exempt the sales tax on retail materials that you buy to create products such as albums, which you then go on to sell. When a retailer or wholesaler sells you specialty papers, stickers, etc., you do not pay tax. You charge your customers the deferred tax when they purchase your products, the custom-made albums. These taxes are then filed quarterly or annually with Uncle Sam.

MERCHANT ACCOUNT

If you're running a home-based business, you may or may not want to bother with credit cards. Let's face it, however—it has become a "plastic" world. If you will be selling products, you may want to consider accepting credit cards; it could impact your sales.

Retail and Internet stores will definitely need to set up a merchant account to process credit card payments. You can look up companies offering this service by typing in "merchant account" in any search engine. Compare fees and services and get the best company geared to your type of business. Fees can vary, so shop carefully. Most fees are roughly 2 to 5 percent and are withdrawn from the customer's payment.

Credit card purchases can require the card be manually swiped through a machine or entered into special computer software, which provides much faster verification that card-swipe machines. The payment is then deposited into your bank account, usually within forty-eight hours, minus the credit card processing fee.

NEED A LOAN?

Finding financing for a business can be tricky. Many new entrepreneurs use their savings, credit cards, or loans from family, or split expenses with a partner. When these ideas are not viable, they usually turn to a bank.

Bank financing is difficult for a new business because start-ups have such a high failure rate, and home-based businesses are always considered unsatisfactory unless you have enough collateral to make it a secured loan rather than an unsecured loan. You might look at a home equity loan or try selling something of value, such as property, a car, etc. Dipping into a 401(k) retirement fund or taking a loan on your life insurance are other options.

"My business plan was the reason I was able to get funding," Penny McDaniel of Legacies LLC told me. "It was also interesting that I was turned down three times by banks when I put my project before a man. A *female* loan officer finally approved me." This is not the first time I've heard of this when pitching an idea that reaches more of a female audience to a bank. Men, due to their lack of interaction with certain markets, don't grasp the impact or appeal. Gentlemen, please put the shotgun down! I confess to knowing nothing about NASCAR and would not understand its appeal *whatsoever!*

If your credit is good, or you've run a different business in the past and can show a track record for revenue and a solid customer base, you might qualify for a personal loan. If you need a vehicle for your business, you may get a little farther finding financing for that. The car or van will act at its own collateral, and at least you can check that one off your "cash needed" list.

Specific types of bank loans, in addition to consumer loans and mortgages, are:

- *Working capital lines* of credit for the ongoing cash needs of the business
- *Credit cards*: higher interest, unsecured revolving credit
- *Short-term commercial loans* for one to three years
- *Longer-term commercial loans*: generally secured by real estate or other main assets
- *Equipment leasing* for assets you don't want to buy outright
- *Letters of credit* for businesses engaged in international trade

Small Business Administration

The Small Business Administration (SBA) is a source you could go to for money. In most cases, the SBA does not do the lending; rather it works with banks and Small Business Investment Companies (SBICs) to guarantee a loan. The SBA has a microloan program that was developed to increase the availability of very small loans to prospective small business owners. The average loan amount is $10,000, with amounts ranging from $100 to $25,000. Once again, the loan is not made directly; instead, you are put in touch with nonprofit intermediaries who make the financial decision and disperse funds.

Venture Capital

Most venture capitalists are looking for a high rate of return, and a speedy one at that. A small start-up business would not be worth their while. Their main interests lay in high-tech businesses or ones with a proven track record or high-impact market. You may find a venture capitalist who is impressed with your credentials or past experience. These are often called "angel" investors, and they may be in a position to see your dream and want to back you. You can find venture capitalists on the Internet by typing in "venture capital," but again, this is probably the last avenue available to a small home-based or retail business.

For any of the above loan ideas, have a well-prepared business plan ready, and a lot of enthusiasm. Enthusiasm for your project can go a long way.

EMPLOYER IDENTIFICATION NUMBER

If you have employees or if you choose a form of business other than a sole proprietorship, have a Keogh plan, or need to withhold income tax, then you will need to contact the IRS to request an Employer Identification Number (EIN). An EIN identifies your business for tax purposes in the same way your social security number identifies you. If you are a sole proprietor, you may simply use your social security number on tax forms and registration materials.

Use Form SS-4 to file for an EIN. These forms are available in post offices, in public libraries, online, or by contacting the IRS. If you are a corporation or a partnership, you must file for an EIN and pay quarterly employment taxes using Form 8109.

You will receive federal tax deposit coupons when you apply for your EIN. Use IRS Publication 505: Estimated Tax Payments and the Estimated Tax Worksheet on Form 10490-ES to figure out how much tax you're likely to pay.

YOUR BUSINESS PLAN

According to Business Filings Incorporated, physically putting a business plan together requires you to translate your thoughts about how you're going to run your business (and how it will perform) into a format that is dictated, in large part, by the business you're in and the expectations of your audience. While most business plans share a similar structure and contain similar information about a business, your business plan will be distinguished by those characteristics that are unique to your business. Just as each person's resume differs because it reflects the particular life experiences of that individual, each business plan will differ. But the format makes it instantly recognizable as a business plan. There is a list of business plan essentials in chapter 12.

The following are the key issues you need to examine before you can actually start to write your plan:

- Audience: Whom are you writing for? If you are writing for third parties outside your business, their needs and expectations will govern the type of information and level of detail in your plan. Your neighborhood banker is going to be far more concerned with the financial performance of your business than with the salary structure you plan for your employees.

- Planning horizon: How far out into the future will your plan extend?

- Type of business: Your business's classification as a service provider, product producer or seller, or mixed provider of products and services will have a huge impact on the type of information in your plan.

- Sources of information: What information is available to you in creating a business plan? How can you reduce the time and effort required to analyze your idea?

- Reasonable assumptions: How can you set yourself up for success by taking a realistic look at internal and external conditions of your business, so as to make reasonable predictions about the future?

Writing Your Business Plan

After you've considered the purpose of your plan and done some background preparation, it's time to implement the actual elements you'll include in a business plan. These do not have to be created in the order shown, although most financial loan officers are accustomed to seeing them in this format:

- Cover page and table of contents: They identify your business and make it easy for the reader to find and examine particular documents.

- Executive summary: This is arguably the single most important part of your document. It provides a high-level overview of the entire plan that emphasizes the factors that you believe will lead to success.

- Business background: This is the section that provides company-specific information, describing the business organization, history, and the product or service the business will provide.

- Marketing plan: This presents an analysis of the market conditions that the business faces, sets forth the marketing strategy that the business will follow, and provides a detailed schedule of marketing activities to support sales. Include competitors in your area and how your business will offer more than they do.

- Action plans: This is where you detail how operational and management issues will be resolved, including contingency planning.

- Financial projections: This is another extremely important section. Your projections (and historical financial information, if you have it) demonstrate how the business can be expected to do financially if the business plan's assumptions are sound.

- Appendix: This is the place to present supporting documents, statistical analyses, product marketing materials, resumes of key employees, etc.

A business plan may seem daunting, but it is totally necessary and will point out the areas where you are weak. You may need to do more research on manufacturers or your competition. Perhaps your management team could be stronger in a given area.

If you are planning to open a retail establishment, a carefully documented business plan is an absolute must. You will need to forecast your income with a *cash flow chart* and *break-even analysis*, so your research into your business is vital.

One very good book available is the *Business Planning Guide* by David H. Bangs, Jr. This is one of the most comprehensive books I've seen on the subject of business planning, complete with sample business plans and existing business overviews. Go to *www.bizfilings.com* for in-depth online help with detailed information on each portion of the business plan.

KNOW YOUR BOOKKEEPING

I realize this chapter has been lengthy and your head is probably spinning. The bottom line is: Your business will require good record-keeping, a head for budgeting and planning, good organizational and people skills, and a desire to keep the government happy. Too many businesses have been shut down due to owners ignoring tax regulations or thinking they could cheat the government.

Take your time figuring out start-up costs. Don't think, "Oh, well, if I run out of money, Aunt Sarah has always loaned me money in the past." This is a business venture now, not a hobby, and it should be treated as such. Figure out the cost of everything you will need in order to open the doors of your business. These are your one-time *start-up expenses*. Now determine how much you think it will cost to run your business on a monthly basis, including employee payroll, inventory, overhead, vehicle expenses, advertising, etc. Finally add in a slush fund, the amount of buffer you've set aside in case of unexpected expenses. This is called a *contingency fund*, and it is vital. Do *not* open your business on your last dime. This is why so many businesses fail. You should ideally have enough set aside to run your business for one year.

Cash flow analysis is so important. It shows how much money is coming in and how much is going out. It will tell you if perhaps you're extending too much credit to customers and unable to pay the monthly bills. Or that you are ordering too much inventory when sales and revenue don't warrant it.

Your *break-even analysis* is your projection of when you believe the business will have generated enough income to pay for the operating expenses—exactly when you expect to break even. Any additional revenue would be profit. FYI: Profit is the goal here!

Your *balance sheet* and profit-and-loss sheets will tell you at a glance how you're doing. Are you in the red or the black? Are you where you thought you would be based on your business plan projections, or ahead or behind? Some businesses are seasonal and will need to hit it hard in their strong months to coast through their slower ones. These two sheets will let you know if you're generating enough to make it.

Our final financial concern is the world of taxes. Wait! Come back! It's not that bad, and the IRS really is a friendly place once you've visited their domain. They've gone to a lot of trouble to make their forms "user-friendly" and put out buckets of literature to hold your hand and walk you through their regulations and requirements. Once you've set up good record-keeping, the rest is a snap. So, hoist up your bootstraps and let's wade on!

THE TAXING WORLD OF TAXES

This is an area many new entrepreneurs took for granted when working for someone else. Your former employer took care of these headaches for you. He withheld federal, state, and perhaps city taxes from your paycheck, as well as social security and Medicare (FICA). He also paid unemployment taxes (FUTA) and reported them dutifully on a W-2 form.

As a self-employed person, whether you are a sole proprietor or in a partnership, you will pay income tax on your net profit, and you will have to pay self-employment tax to cover social security and Medicare. Check with your local governments about specific taxes. Though state and local taxes vary, they generally use your federal tax return to determine your income or loss for a given year.

A state sales tax must be paid based on the sales of supplies and materials charged to the client. You can go to *www.irs.ustreas.gov* to get an overview of what the federal government requires.

The IRS has a great guide called the *Tax Guide for Small Business* (Form 334) that will help you with your Schedule C or Schedule C-EZ if you are a sole proprietor. You will need to attach one of these forms to Form 1040. The tax guide just mentioned will help you determine your tax year, accounting, cost of goods sold, and gross profit and business expenses.

Schedule A lists personal deductions and must also be filled out. If you were a subcontractor for another business, you will be issued Form 1099-MISC at the end of the year.

You will send in quarterly income tax and must estimate what you feel you will earn in one year. Always err on the side of generosity here, or you'll owe Uncle Sam come April 15. The IRS has a helpful publication for this as well (I told you they were user-friendly!) called Form 505, Estimated Tax Payments. These quarterly payments are due April 15, June 15, September 15, and January 15. Form 1040-ES has an estimated Tax Worksheet to help you figure how much you might expect to pay.

Fixed Expenses

If you are working from your home, you are able to claim certain things as deductions on your Income Tax Self-Employed Forms. These include:

- ◉ Rent. The area of your home used *exclusively* for your business. You cannot deduct mortgage or rent paid on the entire house—only the portions used only for business purposes. For instance, if you use the basement *only* for scrapbook workshops, crops, or business inventory, you may deduct that portion of the house payment. An example would be: If you live in a 2,500-square-foot home and your basement area used for your work is 800 square feet, you may use that percentage of your house payment as a deduction. Figure out what percentage 800 square feet of 2,500 is (it's 32 percent) and use that percentage rate as your guide. You would use the same method to determine your utility deductions. Form 8829, Expenses for Business Use of Your Home, is there to help you with your calculations.

- Professional Fees. Accountants, lawyers, money paid for special classes, a professional's advisory fees, a photographer's service, etc., are deductible.

- Advertising and Promotional Costs. Car lettering, Yellow Pages ads, flyers, newspaper ads, business cards, trade show expenses, brochures, etc.

- Capital Investments. Your vehicle, depreciable scrapbook equipment (cutting machines, etc.), and so on are deductible for their depreciation value for that year on your tax forms.

- Utilities. The percentage of heat, gas, lights, water, etc., used in your home exclusively for your business areas can be deducted. Use the same method you used in figuring rent or mortgage deductions.

- Banking. The expense for checks, bank service charges, bad debts, collection costs, etc. used for your business.

- Office Expense. Telephone, supplies, computer, printer, fax, copier, desk, etc. can be deducted once, the year they were purchased. This would include in-home rack displays for your scrapbooking merchandise, work tables, etc. Ask your accountant about depreciation on expensive office equipment.

- Insurance. Your business-related insurance fees are deductible.

Variable Expenses

These are expenses that vary with the amount of work you do:

- Supplies and Materials. All scrapbook supplies, office stationary, invoices, etc. are deductible.

- Hired Helpers. Keep track of hours and payments for anyone you use on a freelance basis for your business.

- Mileage. Keep records of your miles, gas, and maintenance expenses. If your car is used for both personal and business needs, claim only the amount used for business purposes.

- Clothing. Any clothes purchased as your professional wardrobe for your business can be deducted. Be careful with this area and don't abuse it. These calculations should be for business-related purposes only.

Taxes for Retail or Employees Added

If you've reached the point where you would like to hire employees for your home-based business or you are opening a retail outlet, you will take on the joy of added tax responsibilities.

- Withholding FIT. Your employees will fill out a W-4 Form that claims the number of withholding allowances. Use IRS Publication 15 or Circular E to determine the appropriate amount of federal income tax to withhold.

- Withholding FICA. You will withhold social security and Medicare taxes from your employees' paychecks. The percentage to withhold is 6.2 percent for social security for wages up to $65,400 and 1.45 percent for Medicare.

- FUTA Tax is your unemployment tax. You will pay 6.2 percent of your employee's first $7,000 in earnings. This tax return is filed once a year using Form 940, or 940-EZ. This is different from your other filings, as the form is due January 31. Your state will have unemployment tax, and you'll receive credit from the federal government for the state payment.

Form 941 has to do with employee compensation and taxes withheld along with your employer's share of FICA. Use Form 941, Employer's Quarterly Federal Tax Return.

Form W-2 sums up an employee's income and withholding for one year. Your employees must receive copies of these forms no later than January 31. In addition, you must attach the form(s) to Form W-3 and happily send it along to the Social Security Administration.

If you've set your business up as a corporation instead of a sole proprietorship, you will have additional tax responsibilities. Form 1120 is required for corporate income taxes on net profits. Corporate tax rates can range from 15 percent to 30 percent of the business's profits. Corporations also pay for employees' social security and Medicare tax.

We deserve a reward after this chapter: you for reading and absorbing all the information, and me for writing it! Grab a cold soda, rub your eyes, and let's take a look at which arena of the scrapbooking industry you will be tossing your template into. We'll start with the home-based business.

CHAPTER 4

The Home-Based
Scrapbooking Business

*R*unning a business from the comfort and security of your own home has become a nationwide epidemic. With the surge of layoffs, downsizing, and plain old job insecurity, becoming our own boss never looked so tempting. The phrase "cottage industry" is taking on a whole new meaning.

Unstable corporate tendencies are not the only reason people are turning their garages and basements in profit-producing square footage. There is a growing need to return to simpler times and the home—the very reasons scrapbooking has found a resurgence in popularity. Instead of seeking the biggest paycheck, Americans are asking themselves, "Does this make me happy? Is this stress worth the bucks?"

When a home business is based on a craft, hobby, or skill and it produces enough revenue to pay the bills, it is a fabulous feeling. You are making a living at something you create, and that's a hard feeling to beat. For twenty-five years, I banked respectable deposits painting murals and rendering faux finishes. You not only collect monies, but you get the added pleasure of being complimented on your work and having your talent appreciated. There were many times my ego-inflated head did not fit into the van at the end of a day. Compare that to working for someone else, where sadly, the only time you receive attention is when you've done something wrong.

Before you quit your day job, however, first find out if you qualify for a home-based business.

ZONING LAWS

You've been using your home to create elaborate scrapbooks, possibly even had friends over to work on theirs, or taught a class or two for fun. The idea of turning your love into a business has been percolating on your brain's back burner for a while now. How much harder could it be . . . right?

Not all home-based businesses are welcome in neighborhoods by either your neighbors or the zoning commission. Before you order a simple, yet elegant, sign for your front door, you will need to get permission to operate out of your home. You may also require a business license.

Call your city or town hall and find out the regulations for your subdivision or address. If your home sits in an area that is toward the outskirts of town or newly constructed in a part of town that was originally portioned for diverse usage, you may be within a commercially slated area and be allowed to operate a business.

Many people have blown off going before the zoning commissioner and decided to open their business anyway, thinking no one will know since the number of cars is no different from someone having an occasional party. Please don't go there. You can get shut down after all your hard work and expense. Make it legal to start with, and you'll sleep at night.

Variances

If you are declined, don't give up right away. You can apply for a variance, which basically means they will take a close look at your type of business and decide if it is a low-impact home business (no noise, few customers, no hazardous materials, etc.).

Variances can be costly, so look into them ahead of time. Some require legal help. The city may instruct you on how many parking spaces you may have and whether your home requires certain improvements, such as a widened driveway or specially inspected work areas. You may need to petition your neighbors to receive their blessing on your new home venture.

STAYING FRIENDS WITH THE NEIGHBORS

I was raised in a home-based business and have carried on in that time-honored tradition. I have yet to run into a neighbor who did anything but send me business. I have heard some pretty bad horror stories from others, however, regarding unsupportive neighbors.

A friend of mine sells candles and has in-home parties on a routine basis. The woman across the street invariably comes stalking over during one of the candle parties and points out to my friend that "someone's car" is *almost* blocking her driveway. FedEx trucks, UPS, mail packages, etc. are all duly griped about.

When my mother opened a modeling agency in her home many years ago and applied for a zoning permit, she was told to get the signatures of each neighbor in her neighborhood who would be affected by the parked cars during class time. Whether your city requires that or not, it's not a bad idea to talk to your surrounding neighbors and inform them of your business intentions and get their goodwill ahead of time. Crop parties, meetings, and workshops could create a great deal of traffic and parking problems, so think ahead and call your city hall for regulations.

Go the extra mile now to approach your neighbors and describe in detail what business you are hoping to open in your home and what impact, if any, it will have on the neighborhood. If they are told about the number of cars parking in the cul-de-sac and how often, you can learn now how they feel about it. You might ask if any would be willing to accept a delivery should you not be available. Reassure them about the noise level and hours of operation.

Taking a plate of cookies to the neighbors bordering your home, who will receive the brunt of the parking, may not be a bad idea. By obtaining their good will, you might be innocently soliciting business from them and from the friends they tell about you.

SETTING UP DELIVERY SERVICE

We will discuss ordering from manufacturers and how they ship orders in this chapter, but for now, decide where you would like to have packages delivered (front porch, side door, etc.). A friend of mine runs a quilting business from her home, and has a large green Rubbermaid receptacle on the porch by her front door with a sign above it saying, "Please leave all deliveries in the plastic tub. Thank you." I'm assuming her deliveries are not of gigantic proportions, but you get the idea.

Many shipments made to you may have to be signed for. If you are expecting an important delivery and will be away, you may want to arrange for a neighbor to receive it.

Your manufacturer will dictate how and by whom your shipments will be made. Getting on good terms with your UPS or FedEx drivers never hurts. Once they know you well, they may be willing to bend a few rules and leave items for you or make a second trip if they happen to miss you. I'm not advocating exploiting them; just be nice!

THE IN-HOME SHOP

Working from home has many advantages. The morning and afternoon commute can be the time it takes to get from your bedroom to your office. If your office is *in* your bedroom, you won't even have to circle the block.

If you are working from home, you will need "professional space" no matter what part of the scrapbooking vocation you are jumping into. A home office can literally be set up anywhere. You may be lucky enough to have a spare room or section of basement or garage that can be converted into a functional work place. If ingenuity is needed here to find an area for your desk and office requirements, then let's put our minds to it for a moment.

Finding Office Space

Many of my friends are entrepreneurs working from home. They range from interior decorators to financial advisors. I've seen desks in corners of dining rooms, roll-tops doubling as antiques in living rooms, a door straddling two sawhorses in a laundry room, and a cloth-draped kitchen table with all the files and supplies hidden beneath it.

Designating a specified area of your home for business has many advantages, not the least of which is privacy. You're running a business, and it needs to be taken seriously. Members of your family or roommates need to understand your work hours and the importance of respecting your business space. Unfortunately, when your work is scattered across the dining room table, the kids still see you as Mom, and neighbors don't always understand the "I really *am* working here" scenario.

Here's what you can get by with until you have more room, or even if you do have an area of your home stamped "office."

Desk or Filing Cabinet

Keep it simple. You need a place to keep your records, invoices, shipping orders, and correspondence. A file designated for advertising transactions, clippings of your ads, flyers, etc. is a good idea. Additional shelves to hold books on scrapbook ideas, albums, and supplies will also be needed. It would be preferable if you have an entire closet you could set aside for inventory.

Inventory

Adequate storage for your merchandise is very important. You've spent a large sum of money on these items, and having those specialty papers you spent hours picking out crumpled or torn due to being shoved inside a box or beneath a book makes no sense at all—not to mention what it will do to your sales to have damaged goods.

Start now with an organized storage area. Stores like Michaels and Hobby Lobby have those wonderful clear plastic containers for as little as one dollar, complete with lids. Separate your stickers, die cuts, ribbons, brads, etc. into different containers and label them. Nothing feels better than being able to lay your hands on something at a moment's notice, especially with a customer waiting. Put your specialty papers in flat boxes. Sam's Club always has spare boxes piled up at the end of the cash registers. Nab a few flat ones, do some cutting if you need to, and keep your flat items in them.

Home Depot and other hardware stores sell terrific bins to hold small things such as nuts and bolts. These work wonderfully for your tiny embellishments that could get lost. Think outside the box. When looking at containers, don't look at their intended purpose, look at what they *could* be! When painting wall murals, I used fishing tackle boxes for my supplies, and loved the compartments. There are even specially made storage bins just for scrappers. Consult your hobby stores or scrapbooking magazines.

Those wonderful Rubbermaid storage bins on wheels with the see-through drawers are wonderful. You can wheel them to your workshop, place them next to your desk, or push them into a corner or closet.

Stores going out of business usually put their display items up for sale. Card racks, bookcases, display cases can all be bought for next to nothing. Frequent garage sales and look for usable armoires, shelving units, and desks.

When purchasing your inventory and office equipment, "Watch your business expenses," says Sharon Colasuonno, Creative Memories consultant. "Do you really need it, or just *want* it?" Start slow and build. You can really get carried away purchasing inventory—all those pretty baubles that you feel you must have. Create an inventory budget and stick to it. If a customer needs some specialty item, you can always buy it for her then.

Computer

Every business needs a computer. You will need one not only for bookkeeping, but also for researching manufacturers, surfing scrapbooking Web sites, possibly creating your Web site, being accessible to e-mail from customers and vendors, and (ahem) peeking at your competition. You can also buy wonderful software that enables you to create your own letterhead stationery, business cards, advertising flyers and brochures, even small signage. Newsletters to your customers can be professionally rendered, and let's not forget mailing lists and customer tracking ability.

Phone and Answering Service

My first word of advice here is to have a separate line for your business. I tried for years to get along with my home phone and business line being one and the same, and it was a nightmare. Not only did I have to fight with teenage sons who "had to make just one more phone call, Mom," but the Internet was also tied to it, so calls were logged on an answering machine and retrieved *much* later. An additional line does not cost that much more a month, and it is worth every penny for the stress it will relieve. If you can, put your Internet on a cable hookup rather than phone to keep your business line free. True, your Internet service provider now offers call alert, which allows you to see who and when someone is trying to reach you by phone while you're online. That's helpful if you're going to stay with a phone modem hookup.

Make sure your phone message is professional and brief—a simple, "You have reached Alluring Albums. I am away from my office. Please leave a detailed message, phone number, and a good time to reach you. Thank you for your call."

If you are using your phone for both business and family, try "Hello. You have reached the Flagman residence and Alluring Albums. Please leave a message after the beep and we'll return your call as quickly as we can. Thank you." You can get voice messaging that allows the caller to choose a family member's name by pressing the designated number on the keypad. For instance, "If you wish to speak to Michael, please press 1; if you wish to speak to Marsha with Alluring Albums, press 2."

Call waiting is a must if you don't want to miss calls while your daughter Alissa complains to Sharon how "like awful" Marie is being and how "totally lame" she was at the party.

Return calls promptly. Customers shop around, especially if they're in a hurry and don't want to wait on a needed item or service. Someone may need to firm up a budget for a wedding album by late afternoon. A quick response is even more important if you are dealing with a disgruntled customer.

Fax Machine/Copier

Commercial clients will ask for information to be faxed to them, or will want to fax changes and updates to you. Get a fax machine that has a copier to save money. Always keep copies of correspondence, orders, designs, and bids. It avoids misunderstandings down the road, and gives you a ready reference to contact when memory fails. You can order a distinctive ring for your fax that allows you to have a separate phone number to hand out as your fax number. When a fax comes in, the ring will allow you to distinguish it from a voice call.

Printer and Scanner

A printer is obviously a must to go along with your computer.

These are so affordable now that they hardly put a dent in your office equipment budget. Shop for good clarity, and make sure it's compatible with your computer.

Scanners are not a necessity, but I use mine frequently. They allow you to scan almost anything in two-dimensional format, import it to your computer, and either print it, e-mail it, or add it to your Web site. You could scan an album page layout idea for a customer and e-mail it to her.

Cell Phone

Ah, yes, the bane of the civilized man. Do we love them, or hate them?

Well, folks, I will stand bravely before you and admit I'd be lost without them. They give me peace of mind that my children can reach me when I'm away, or a panicked client can track me down. A last-minute change in an important order can be handled before I return home to find it waiting in a buried voice message.

If you're going to a meeting or delivery for the first time and you get lost, the cell phone enables you to call for directions and be told you passed the correct exit while you were admiring the Cadillac Escalade in the lane next to you. Roadside emergencies are another biggie.

Camera

An office supply you may not have thought of is a camera. Taking pictures of your displays and creations to create a portfolio is a must. A digital camera will allow you to upload pictures onto the Internet and use them as needed for customers, vendors, trade shows, etc. You can also create brochures and other advertising items with your pictures.

Office Supplies

You don't need much in the way of office supplies to begin your in-home business. Letterhead stationery, invoices, business cards, printer paper, paper clips, stapler, pens, pencils, a Rolodex for customer names and information, notebooks, and envelopes. You can buy more as your needs demand. A calendar or Day-Timer is a must for appointments, workshop schedules, and delivery dates. A dry-erase board over our desk is great to note deliveries and to schedule classes and crops.

If you want to be super-organized, buy a smaller dry-erase board to post near your work area, informing your family of class times and work hours for that day. It is a huge help, instead of reminding them six times that you will not be available from 6 to 8 P.M. due to a workshop in the basement.

Workshop Areas

When first starting out, most home-based scrapbookers use whatever is available for work areas. The most common place is a dining room or kitchen table.

"Workshops and crops can be held at the dining room table," Suzi Moran of Creative Memories told me. "It's intimate and handy. If you need more space, folding tables from the garage can be brought in to expand the area. If you live in an apartment complex, you might be able to use the complex's community room for your classes and crops."

Suzi had some other wonderful ideas for me. "Until three years ago, I did everything from home. Now, due to a larger client base, I use a community room at a local realty office. These rooms are usually available for nonprofit organizations only, but if you ask nicely or have a friend in the realty business, you may be able to schedule the room."

She went on to say that if you're networking with other scrapbook consultants and need more space, you can have a customer city-wide conference and split the cost of a rented venue area. Most rented rooms will run you around $150 or less.

You can get inventive and have outdoor workshops on picnic tables, or dress up the garage with fun displays and colorfully draped folding tables. Your customers are there to work on their albums, buy products, or swap ideas. The surroundings do not have to be conference-room perfect.

To set up your work area, you will need all the supplies necessary for scrapbook workshops, crops, meetings, and sales parties. Having everything in organized containers or display racks and cases is very important. Don't waste customer time looking for misplaced items. There is a wonderful book that covers everything you'll need for scrapbooking, called *The Complete Idiot's Guide to Scrapbooking*. It is wonderfully illustrated and very comprehensive. The pages are stuffed with page layout ideas and clever use of embellishments. Since the main objective of this book is to teach you how to open and operate an in-home business, I won't go into the techniques and actual creation of albums. There are many good books out there on those subjects.

FAMILY SUPPORT

I've run a home-based business for over twenty-five years now. From pregnancy to full-grown sons, I've worked around every obstacle you can imagine. Once, while running an advertising agency from my home, I was painting a twenty-five-foot vinyl banner in the basement for a bank that needed it the next morning to carry in a parade. I had just finished the last touch of green enamel when the phone rang upstairs. I set down my brush and bolted up the stairs. My two-year-old son was supposed to be outside with his father working on a garden bed. I finished the phone call and heard giggling coming from the basement. In horror, I raced down two flights of steps to see my little boy running barefoot down the length of my banner, wet green enamel paint shining from the soles of his feet. I did the worst thing I could have done: I shouted, "*Brandon!*" and he bolted—off the banner and onto the white carpet. By the time I snatched him up, there were tiny green footprints down the entire length of my project, and several more looking like a morose treasure map across the family room rug. The footprints would not come off the banner, no matter how much turpentine or lacquer thinner I used. All I came away with was a serious buzz. The bank fired me, my husband hugged me, and my son proudly held up his shamrock-green-stained feet to all who would see them.

If you're through laughing at my expense, I will explain now that getting your family's support is all-important. Explain the benefits of your new job: more income, happy Mommy, happy Daddy (who has just been relieved of the title of sole provider), and happy customers whose lives you're enriching. Chances are the last one won't mean a whole lot to them, but the extra income and a stab at Disneyland will.

Explain the phone rules, office privacy conditions, noise, helping with household chores, and keeping the house tidy for drop-in customers. It's a good idea to reward their efforts to help out. A Family Appreciation Night is a great way to say, "Thank you for supporting my dream!"

"Get your husband's and family's support from the get-go," Suzi Moran of Creative Memories declares. "It is all-important."

I was raised in a modeling agency run out of our home, and the rules I had to follow were:

1. No cut-offs during business hours.

2. No chewing gum during business hours.

3. No curlers during business hours.

4. Answer the phone with the business name, not just, "HALL-LOOOOO?"

5. No loud TV during . . . yep, business hours.

6. No cooking in the kitchen during . . .

7. No tying up the phone, yadda, yadda, yadda.

8. No boyfriends parking their cars in the driveway to block the models.

9. No interrupting Mom during class time unless you've just singed your eyebrows off.

   And last but not least . . .

10. No mistaking the facial cream in the refrigerator for mayonnaise. (Tip for you women: Cosmetics kept in the refrigerator will close your pores and give a smoother appearance! You're welcome.)

One last word about your work area: Don't forget that your car is an extension of your business. You will be making deliveries, buying inventory, and attending meetings.

Make sure your business is well represented with a clean, uncluttered vehicle. If you open the door and a month's worth of McDonald's wrappers waft their way down the street, this does not give the impression of an organized profession. We will discuss car lettering as a good adverting idea in chapter 10.

CHECKING OUT THE COMPETITION

While building your business plan, find out who your competition really is. You won't just be looking at other home-based scrapbook businesses, but at retail and Internet stores as well. Your client base will shop around, so you will have to offer something your competitor doesn't, whether it is in the guise of better prices, better customer service, or both.

I feel your advantage is in the ability to offer your customer the "down-home" personal touch. You not only work in surroundings that scream "home, hearth, and family" (all the things scrapbook albums are centered around), but you have time to give your clients your personal attention—something the Internet cannot do and most retail stores are too busy to do.

Most retailers offer newsletters that are sent out on a regular basis to announce classes, sales, and upcoming events. Collect these and study them. What can you do better? Can you offer business hours at night or on days your competition is closed, to accommodate the customers who work during the day or want to shop on Sundays? How about some creative package deals your other home-based competitors aren't offering that would save your client money? Would you be willing to do crop parties in a customer's home or make special deliveries and rush orders?

Be sure to do your research in pricing. Go to the hobby stores like Michaels and Hobby Lobby and specialty scrapbook stores. Target and other department stores are also offering supplies in this exploding industry. The Internet can sell merchandise without the overhead costs, so online sellers can price their wares lower. Can you compete?

Pull in the Internet buyers by pointing out they can handle and inspect your merchandise and buy it immediately without the wait or shipping costs. When you are going up against online and retail shops, you must offer better service to overcome their lower prices due to their buying in bulk, etc. Do your homework!

The key to building a solid client base is to offer more, whether in goods or services. One thing I always did in my painting business was to leave behind a small thank-you gift voicing my appreciation for the privilege of being in the clients' home and the income they provided me. The gift always centered on the project we did, and was a welcome surprise and finishing touch. For instance, if I rendered their kitchen in an Italian Tuscany faux finish, I found beautiful oil and vinegar bottles and presented them with a loaf of fresh home-baked bread on a red linen napkin along with a note.

If your client places an order with you, perhaps you could throw in an extra brad or a sheet of paper with a brand-new page design and layout idea that centers on her project. Send a card on her birthday and a cupcake on her child's birthday, or start an incentive program where she receives a grab-bag of goodies for every dollar amount in sales reached or for pulling her name from a hat. Use those creative juices and build a business clients can't refuse.

I would like to add this warning from David Kovanen with Addicted to Scrapbooking and Addicted to Rubber Stamps, two highly successful Internet store sites: "As for encouraging individuals to start a home-based business, I have mixed thoughts. Persons that offer something unique could succeed. But most persons we are aware of who try to start an online scrapbooking company fail miserably for the simple reason that this niche is already highly saturated with similar companies. Persons often have the simplistic notion that they can purchase products at wholesale, then just open up a Web site, and they will have a thriving business. I know several people who have lost their savings doing exactly that.

"To succeed, you must think about inventory control, fulfillment efficiency, purchasing, replenishment, inbound freight, and so on. To put it more bluntly: Why would customers shop from your site when our company offers a selection of more than 250,000 products, overnight delivery, toll-free customer service, and a host of other advantages?

"I am saddened by the dashed dreams, false hopes, and disillusion-ment that many of these entrepreneurs have from thinking that they will happily spend all of their time scrapbooking on the job, rather than worrying about how to install ultraviolet protectors on their light bulbs to keep their inventory from yellowing and turning old before it is even sold."

I would like to thank David for his candor and concern. I will have more about David and his businesses in chapter 6, The Electric

Entrepreneur. For now, these are things to consider before investing your money. Again, you have to be creative in establishing a solid client base.

WHOLESALE DISTRIBUTORS

As we mentioned before, many manufacturers are hesitant to do business with you. Why? Because they feel your home-based business and the increase in Web sites hurts the brick-and-mortar stores trying to run a business. Plus, they feel your small, new setup will not bring the bulk inventory orders that larger establishments will. The cost of them sending you their catalogues, invoicing, and advertising materials may seem a waste of time and resources based on your order volume. Here are the steps you need to take to try to get these manufacturers to take you seriously:

Contact the manufacturer or supplier you found on the Internet or through scrapbook and hobby magazines, and ask for their wholesale prices. They will probably want your tax resale number and other evidence that you are in a true business. Provide evidence of your good credit history and offer to make special payment arrangements until you have established a good track record with them.

Shop around and check out other manufacturers' prices and delivery promises. Collect catalogues and magazines and compare company policies and sales promotions.

You might consider networking with other scrapbook home businesses, and thus ordering in bulk and splitting the profits. The Web is full of scrapbook opportunities, including groups; *www.groups.yahoo.com* offers Scrapbooking4others and 4scrapbookretailers, which invite you to participate in group purchases with other people in the scrapbook business.

Researching on the Internet should give you a lot of ideas of what manufacturers are offering and what your potential competition is up to. You can't gather *enough* information before opening your doors.

The distributors will tell you how they ship, which shipping company you will be receiving your merchandise from, and the charge. You have little control in this area.

Talk to them about the best times to order, and whether bulk orders will receive special pricing or possibly smaller shipping prices. Don't be afraid to ask questions. One manufacturer with stringent, unyielding rules might not be as helpful as another who is willing to work with you. Shop around. The larger companies usually take longer to ship orders. Ask!

STAYING PROFESSIONAL

Let's face it: There are down sides to working from your home. I just experienced one ten minutes ago. I heard a splash and "Oops!," and looked outside my office door to find my hardwood floors soaking wet. My teenage son and his friends had been having a water-balloon fight out back when one of them opened the door to the house at the precise moment a loaded missile was lobbed. It entered through the door, hit the floor, and exploded.

You will have interruptions from the phone, the dog, the neighbors, a hungry husband, telephones, doorbells, and cats walking across your keyboard until the invoice you were typing now looks like this: kouohok-fsadoiylgljasy oyohdf.

However, your family will quickly sense it if you take yourself seriously as a professional. Set up your terms and regulations *now*. This is a business, not a hobby. They would no more go down to Daddy's office and tie up the phone or use the Internet to download movie prices from Fandango than eat eggplant casserole. Set business hours and enforce them. Gently let friends and neighbors know the times you are working and not to be disturbed. Have customers call ahead and not just drop by. Let your family know which areas are *off limits* and not to be touched. Your specialty papers are not for homework use unless you've been asked. The scissors, rulers, paste, etc., do *not* leave the workshop area. And, finally, phone time (if you are operating off a shared line) is regulated, and courtesy is used when addressing your customers.

Have the laundry caught up or hidden, the floors vacuumed, and the dishes done if customers are expected. It's a good practice whether you expect them or not. During class time, have the television off or turned way down. That goes for stereos and stomping kids. Remember, I told you to get your family's support ahead of time.

CREATIVE MEMORIES

For the scrapbook enthusiast who wants to build a home-based business but would rather have all the background work done for her ahead of time, Creative Memories is a boon to this market.

Creative Memories is one of the fastest-growing direct-sales companies in the United States. They provide profitable career opportunities for those who believe in and want to share the Creative Memories mission and values with others.

"Our consultants enhance our customers' lives," states Sharon Colasuonno, a Creative Memories consultant who has a wonderful home-based business. Her basement workshop area is very professionally done. "We're reinforcing their memories. I'm still educating people about their albums," she states. "What it means for a paper to be acid-free, etc."

As a Creative Memories consultant, you are an independent businessperson selling Creative Memories products with the support of a company that stands behind you as you grow your business. You'll receive training to provide customers with advice on how to use the products and share the features and benefits of the product and techniques. The consultant kit costs only $195. It includes all the tools you will need to complete your demo album, schedule home classes and shows, and more. The income potential is unlimited and grows with your recruiting ability. You can get full information at *www.creativememories.com*.

You can also check out Sharon Colasuonno's Web site at *www.CreativeMemories.com/SharonColasuonno*, or visit Suzi Moran, a Creative Memories Unit Manager I met, at *www.CreativeMemories.com/SuziMoran*. These women were wonderful in helping me understand the home-based potential of scrapbooking and the groundbreaking work Creative Memories has done for this industry. If you like having someone else do the original brainstorming and you would like to jump on board their bandwagon, go to *www.MyMommyBiz.com* for a wealth of information on franchises for home-based businesses in the scrapbooking industry.

A final word on the subject of running a business from your home: There will be grumbling. I grumbled at my mother that our home was no longer a home, but a business. Don't let it hurt your feelings. Address it, compromise where you can, and be strong where you can't. Point out again the benefits of the extra income and a mother who goes after her dreams.

Now, if you'll excuse me, I have to go mop a floor.

CHAPTER 5

Going Retail

*I*f owning your own store is more appealing to you than working from home, I can only assume you know the demand of the retail industry. With the daunting figure of 60 percent of new businesses failing in the first year, it always impresses me when the determined entrepreneur plunges ahead with her dreams anyway.

In order to determine whether you have a viable business prospectus, you must have completed a thorough business plan and covered every area. There is no hedging in this all-important start-up overview. By really investigating each area we covered in the section on business plans, you will feel a peace of mind that you are ready, that you have the necessary funds (including a substantial buffer), and that you know your competition, your target market, and your inventory inside out.

"I spent over a year researching the scrapbook retail market before I approached a bank for a business loan," Penny McDaniel of Legacies LLC told me. Penny runs a very successful scrapbooking retail store in Loveland, Colorado. "What you expect and what you plan for are not necessarily what you get," she cautions. Doing your homework helps eliminate the really costly mistakes that can sink you before your first customer enters the door.

That said, let's see what you can expect.

THE PROS AND CONS

Obviously, one of the main *pros* to opening a retail site is the income potential. You are able to increase inventory and thus (hopefully) sales. You perhaps have an area for a workshop; workshops generate revenue and increase product sales. Your ability to offer innovative ideas, classes, holiday specials, etc., has more impact due to the clout that owning a retail outlet gives you over a home-based setup. You have more money for advertising and may own a Web site as well.

Manufacturers are more willing to work with you as a retail concern; you are now in a position to "wheel and deal," or jockey for better shipping rates and bulk discounts. Costly catalogues are dutifully dispatched to your door, along with sales incentives.

Jeanna Maire with Your Crop Shop of Arvada, Colorado, says, "In my opinion, there is no other way to run this business besides a retail site. By going retail, we have the products available for the customer to touch and feel." This is an obvious advantage over the Internet store sites. "The interaction between us and the customer is great because we're available to assist them whenever they may need us," Jeanna adds. Information about Your Crop Shop can be found at *www.yourcropshop.com*.

Depending on the number of hours you are willing to work and the profit you are able to "plug back" into your business, you can achieve any reasonable goal you've set for yourself.

Speaking of hours worked, we now enter the *cons* arena. Most successful scrapbook business owners work an average of forty to sixty hours a week, especially in the beginning, when the cost of employees is too prohibitive or they feel a need to oversee the operations personally. Be sure now that you can handle that kind of workload and stress. Multitasking takes on a whole new meaning when you open a retail business.

"The cons are few," Jeanna Maire states. "One may be that the scrapbooking industry is booming, and keeping up with all the latest products and having the room and bucks to stock them is very tough. What we think might sell could be completely the opposite."

Most entrepreneurs feel that if they can run a successful home-based business, they can segue easily into retail. Au contraire! Besides the business of funding (a rather large detail to be considered), you will also need to become an expert on real estate in a brief period of time. Checking out store sites, measuring space, and haggling over lease agreements, zoning laws, and sign allotment are only a few of the headaches in store.

When you take on a lease site, it will come in one of three forms: new construction, existing store site, or existing site in need of remodeling.

New Construction

New construction gives you a wider range of design options, but also many decisions to make. Technically termed a *vanilla shell*, a brand-new site will be a bare-bones minimum.

"You will get the perimeter walls up and dry-walled," according to Peter Kast of Realtec Commercial Realty in Fort Collins, Colorado. "You may or may not get a suspended ceiling; the downside being you cannot have your heating or air conditioning distributed without a suspended ceiling. You will receive an electrical panel, but not necessarily distributed electrical outlets. Your walls will be taped, but not painted, and a vanilla shell does not include floor covering."

As you can see, there is a lot of expense involved with a new site. If you want any kind of partition walls, you will either design these yourself or hire an architect to help you with the placement of walls, bathrooms, work areas, etc.

Penny McDaniel of Legacies LLC emphasized knowing who your neighbors are if you are looking into setting up shop in a strip mall or plaza. "No one should be competing with you, even on a subtle basis," she stated. Find out if any store in the mall is selling albums or photographic embellishments. If you offer a professional photographer as an added service, make sure there is not a photography studio within the plaza's perimeter. This should be included in your lease agreement.

"Lock in your lease for at least three years," Penny cautioned. "This locks them into a lease price that can't escalate on you."

When asked what she saw as the biggest problem resulting in businesses closing their doors, she said, "Undercapitalization"!

Existing Site

If you are looking at an existing store front, you will probably save a lot of money over incorporating your ideas into a new construction location. An existing site will have the walls finished, flooring, lighting, bathrooms, etc. You may not like the wall color, but paint is inexpensive. Perhaps the green and pink linoleum is not to your liking, and you decide to peel it up and go with the new trend in color-glazed cement. The bathrooms may need a little updating, and the microwave the previous owner left behind was probably purchased during the *Brady Bunch* era. These are all fairly minor expenses.

Put your finishing touch on it, erect your shelves and racks, throw down a colorful welcome mat at the door, and it feels like it's been yours all along.

Read your lease carefully. What may have worked for the business just vacating the premises does not necessarily work for you. Watch the parking arrangements, sign allotment, and operating hours. You may want evening hours for workshops, but the landlord does not want the security responsibility.

"You need to be a strong negotiator," Penny McDaniel states. "Hit what insurance the landlord will cover and what *you're* expected to cover hard! In case of water damage from the store next to you, is that *your* insurance responsibility or the landlord's?"

Existing Site Remodeled

You may decide on an existing site, but the walls are in the wrong place and you need an additional work area for classes. You may want two bathrooms instead of one, or a sink area in the workspace for cleanup. This requires remodeling, and may include an architect and his subsequent fees. The landlord will probably have covenants you will have to comply with concerning whether you and your handyman brother-in-law Ralph can do the remodeling yourself, or if you're required to have a licensed contractor.

The city or county governing your location will need to pass inspection on your work before, during, and after, and the health department and fire commissioner will also need to give you the nod. Materials used in the remodel will have to comply with any number of regulations, and if they don't, they will shut you down . . . believe me!

While painting murals for new construction, I saw all sorts of horrific things including being shut down the night before the store opening due to illegal wiring in the walls. It pays to get it done right with a contractor or at least hire one to act as a consultant.

Decide now if a play area for children would be worth the extra expense of partitioning off an area secure enough to make parents comfortable that their little ones are safe. Most retail scrapbook owners told me it *did* pay off for them, and their sales increased due to the fact mothers and fathers could shop without hassle or fear of their toddlers pulling things off the racks. Less stress, more time to buy!

A final word about store sites: It may not be worth your while to set up shop in a space that is too small in an effort to save money. By small, we are talking 1,000 square feet or less. The commercial realtors I interviewed recommended at least 2,000 feet or better in order to stock adequate inventory and provide classes, demonstrations, a child's play area, etc. Don't forget handicapped regulations for door, bathroom, and aisle clearance. If you don't have the funding for adequate space, perhaps you should continue to run your business from your garage or basement for a while longer. You don't want to sink your entire investment into a site that is undersized or in a poor location.

SELECTING A SITE: YEP . . . LOCATION

There is no one in this day and age who has not heard the spiel about the importance of location for a retail business or restaurant; your success or failure can ride entirely on the shoulders of this one business element.

Several factors can help you determine a poor location. Perhaps the store once stood in a busy area of town, but the perimeters have changed and it now resides on the outskirts or in a dilapidated location. The fact that you can get it cheaply is not an incentive. There's a *reason* its price is reduced! Perhaps the store is not easily accessible to traffic. Busy intersections can be a plus or minus. While the exposure is wonderful, it may be a nightmare to find an easy turn lane into your parking lot. Ask other stores at that juncture how the traffic has affected their business; would they choose that location if they had it to do over again?

Jeanna Maire of Your Crop Shop said she chose her location because "We wanted our location to be on a busy intersection, with lots of traffic; plus, we liked the idea that there were a lot of schools around us." She went on to say, "Our store sits a little far off the road, and we are hidden from the main drag by a bank. We would like to have more anchors for our shop, such as restaurants, stores, etc. Our location has served us well, but we hope to make a move in the near future."

We have a brand-new building at a major intersection down the street from us that was constructed four years ago. No one ever moved in. Why? A major drugstore chain built it wanting to profit from the visibility and traffic flow, only to find out after they built it that the two accesses to the parking lot were a mess. Neither traffic direction could enter into it without practically circling the block. So, there it sits.

If you have a site in mind, spend some time parked in front of it and notice the foot traffic. What time of day is it heaviest? What about evening hours? How is the parking? Are people circling the lot trying to find a place to park? Is the building in good repair? Do you like the style of the building and the signage allowed? Many plazas and strip malls will dictate if you can use channel letters, Plexiglas backlit signs, or neon. Your logo may be more conducive to a different sign format. We will talk more about that under "Signage" in this chapter.

If you are buying or leasing an existing site, have a building inspector evaluate it. You don't need to have the added expense of hidden repairs and faulty wiring after you've moved in.

The "How's the Competition" section in this chapter will also come to bear on your location decision.

OVERHEAD

You will need to determine your operating budget based on many things, including your store overhead expenses. These include rent, gas, lights, CAM (maintenance of parking lot and grass, window-cleaning, and snow removal) and insurance. These are fixed expenses that don't vary month to month.

Variable expenses, such as payroll for your employees, advertising, inventory purchases, legal fees, consulting charges from outside professional guidance, and special promotions, can fluctuate. You may decide you only need help part-time one month, but take on full-time help during holiday seasons. Your advertising budget may vary along with your revenue.

If you are in a mall setup, your lease will determine many of your overhead costs. Read it carefully.

HOW'S THE COMPETITION?

Your first thought when it comes to identifying the competition may be to look up other scrapbooking stores in your Yellow Pages within a thirty-mile radius. Although it's helpful to get a fix on specialty scrapbook stores in your vicinity, these are not your only competitors. Craft stores such as

Hobby Lobby and Michaels have entire aisles of merchandise geared to the scrapper. Department stores such as Target, Kmart, and Wal-Mart offer supplies as well. These giants can afford to run sales and discount merchandise due the bulk rates they receive.

What about the Internet? As of this printing, the Internet was not accountable or restricted by sales tax laws, and its operating hours are 24/7. Internet merchants also offer specialty touches such as page layout designs, new product overview, and customer networking with other scrappers. Can you compete with the enormous amount of product they sell? Their downside is that the customer cannot touch or examine the merchandise, check for true color, or "eyeball" sizes and shapes. That's where you come in.

There are some very successful direct-sales companies out there, such as Creative Memories, that are making a huge impact on the scrapbook merchandise buying public. With in-home workshops, sales parties, and outstanding customer service, they are a force to be reckoned with.

Finally, there are catalogue companies such as *Current* that offer orders by mail; home shopping from television programs; and, of course, your in-home business entrepreneur with a fire in his belly to make a mark for himself in the scrapbooking community.

"What is your competition *not* offering?" Penny McDaniel from Legacies LLC asks. "What hours are they offering? Can you capitalize on that? We're open until nine at night, and Sundays; most competitors aren't."

Jeanna Maire of Your Crop Shop states, "We had nothing on this side of town. The closest store was a fifteen-to-twenty-minute drive away."

I asked Jeanna how she researched her competition, and she said, "We try and go to visit the competition as much as we can, or we have one of the employees do it for us."

Janel with The Paper Attic in Sandy, Utah, advised me to tell my readers to "collect your competitor's newsletters and study their class schedules, workshop topics, operating hours, and specials. Are they doing anything unique?"

Penny McDaniel also commented on the benefit of collecting competitors' newsletters to study the advantages they offered their customers. Newsletters through direct mailings are very popular and generate a good rate of customer reaction.

"Look at their store and note aisle space and layout," Janel advises. "Does it look cramped, dark, and unwelcoming? Is the layout confusing, with things bunched in illogical groupings?"

"We listened to our customers and what they were asking for," Janel went on to say.

"They wanted preconstructed, themed idea packs so that it was a no-brainer for them to construct well thought-out pages all coordinated and ready to go. We listen and rotate ideas based on popularity."

Listening to your customers is an often neglected area of business. Instead of hearing complaints, try listening for ideas for improvement that will put you ahead of your competition.

"The Kids' Center is a result of customer interaction," Janel offered. "It is gated and locked, and has a TV, VCR, and toys. These kids are telling their parents *they* want to come to our store," she laughs. "It doesn't get any better than that."

Jeanna Maire explained some of the wonderful innovations that set Your Crop Shop apart from the competition: "We offer specials such as B.O.G.O. (Buy One Get One) Tuesdays for all of our papers. Senior Wednesdays save our customers 15 percent on their purchases made that day. Also, B.O.G.O. Thursdays offer deals on all roll stickers. I don't know of any store that offers this. We've been offering it for over nine months now. We also have three to four large sales a year, which offer huge savings and unbelievable deals. Another edge is that we only have one store and our customers know us well. One of the managers is usually there working. We are on a first-name basis with many of our customers and have developed friendships with them. Women run the shop, and we relate to our largely female customer base."

Defining your competition's strengths and weaknesses is a critical calculation in beginning a new business. Study their inventory and store lay-out as well as location, operating hours, access to residential areas, schools, etc. If they are offering a volume of merchandise you can't possibly compete with, you may want to rethink investing your money in a smaller enterprise. Wouldn't you rather shop where you had more selection, despite the fact the sweet lady at Picture Paste-Ups is offering homemade cookies with each purchase? Find out all you can about your competition before you sign on the dotted line of a lease agreement.

EMPLOYEES

If you can afford to hire employees and you take your time getting the right people for the right job, then by all means do it. A retail business is very demanding, and you'll need time to recharge your batteries. Working long hours alone with no reprieve is mentally and physically draining; your business will suffer for it, and so will your health.

Many new entrepreneurs turn to family, friends, and other enthusiastic scrappers to staff their store. This had its advantages and disadvantages, as we mentioned earlier.

"Our employees have been great!" enthused Jeanna Maire of Your Crop Shop. "They are definitely a blessing. We have gone outside the box by hiring friends, neighbors, and even great customers to work for us. Some say not to do this, but I think, who better to trust and give you reliability than your friends? The time off is also a great perk since the business is very demanding."

Of course, there is a flip side to hiring relatives and friends. Friendships can be ruined and family connections strained when communication falters and responsibilities slip. If you are going to use employees who fall inside your personal circle, I would recommend an in-depth meeting where everyone is told under no uncertain terms what is expected of them, when, and the repercussions if store regulations are not met. Who is in charge of inventory stacking and tracking? Who teaches the workshops and at what times? Who closes up, orders the coffee filters, sweeps the floor, greets the customers, etc.?

You want employees who are eager to be there and who pass that enthusiasm on to the customer. Nothing infuses a shopper with energy more than a happy, upbeat environment where it is clear the love of scrapbooking is abundant. Hire people who know their stuff and who offer the customer ideas and information based on tools and techniques they have actually tried. We've all been in stores where the employee clearly knew nothing concerning the product we were inquiring about and was doing everything not to yawn.

I'm a strong believer in rewarding a job well done. The morale of your business depends largely on you and how you treat your staff. Keep it a great place to come to work and they will return the favor with loyalty and devoted service. Never address a problem with an employee in front of a customer. It is demeaning to the staff and shows a lack of professionalism to the shopper. Handle things discreetly behind closed doors, and always listen to the employee's account of the situation. You may not have all the information concerning the problem.

You will find tax information concerning employees is in chapter 3, Setting Up Shop.

DISPLAY DOS AND DON'TS

I really appreciated the insight I gained on the tried and tested methods of setting up aisles and display cases, which the talented women I interviewed shared with me.

Janel with The Paper Attic had this to say about displaying merchandise: "Obviously, you group the like items together: die-cuts, templates, ribbons, etc. We organize the papers by company so that we know what's running low."

Other scrapbooking store owners I talked to said they grouped their specialty papers by theme and color. This area is a matter of preference, and time will tell you which method works better.

Penny McDaniel of Legacies LLC advises to carefully think of wall placement and display cases in terms of theft. "You need good visibility of the entire store from your cash register area," she states. "I learned after we opened our doors that things were being taken in an area not visible to the store front due to a protruding wall. I removed the wall and the problem."

Display end caps can be used to advertise the aisle contents behind them. "End caps are themed, with a representative sample of what is on that aisle," Janel told me. "For instance, one end cap may be themed toward weddings and show a good selection of what we offer along with some clever decorating ideas. If you don't see exactly what you wanted on the end cap, you can go down the aisle and look at the other wedding merchandise."

Janel places her ideas atop the aisles and end caps where you look up and see colorfully decorated boards. "We use cork boards suspended from the ceiling with hooks. You can find everything from ideas to use with the product on that aisle to upcoming classes and workshops."

"We have eight aisles, fifteen feet long each," Janel said. "The width of the aisles was carefully considered to accommodate strollers and yet keep the merchandise out of reach of the toddlers *in* those strollers. We came up with five to six feet wide as the most effective aisle width."

"We're very proud of our store and its open feeling," she continued. "I've been in stores where the displays made you feel trapped inside the store—no breathing room! A cluttered flow-through can make you feel slightly agitated and pressed in on."

Jeanna Maire of Your Crop Shop says, "It's best to space the displays to flow and to also give the customer a good view of new product. It's nice to order a display from the manufacturer specially made for the product you're selling. It makes it much easier and looks more professional."

"I did not want wire racks," Penny McDaniel told me. "The wood displays look more polished, and they're sturdier. Never underestimate what a child will try to climb! I wanted a layout that allows a comfortable traffic flow."

In terms of placing the merchandise, all the owners I spoke with said to place items, especially new stock, at eye level. "Don't put the product too close to the floor," Penny told me. "From the knees down, you lose visibility."

One idea for what to do with the area that falls inside that lower level range is to place clearance bins there, or other "contained" items, such as plastic craft totes to organize supplies or boxes of remnants left over from classes and workshops marked to sell cheaply. That way, the shelves that are well below the customer's eye level contain items that still catch the eye because they don't lie completely flat. Just be careful they don't protrude into the aisle, where they may be tripped over or strollers can hit them.

"Customers follow a certain pattern," Penny McDaniel told me. "Ninety percent of the people go to the right when they enter a store. Consider that with your traffic flow and learn to direct the 'energy' throughout the store."

Don't forget handicap accessibility when designing aisles and displays. Consider your elderly clientele: Can they reach things, and do you have carts or baskets? Have you provided a children's play area or other ideas that make your store user-friendly?

Notice the traffic pattern and if people are bumping into things or constantly asking directions in order to find items. How is the lighting? Is it dark, or is it well lit and inviting? Do they have a workshop area, and if so, how many can they seat?

Overhearing conversations between shoppers provides a wealth of information concerning their likes and dislikes about the store.

BUSINESS HOURS

"Our hours are very flexible for the customer," Jeanna Maire states. "We are open seven days a week! Our operating hours are Monday through Saturday, 10 to 7 P.M., and Sunday is 12 to 5 P.M. We just realized we needed to be open and accommodating for the busy mother, etc. These hours work well for most."

The Paper Attic in Sandy, Utah, has operating hours of 10 to 7 P.M. on Mondays and 10 to 9 P.M. Tuesdays through Saturdays. With the Mormon population in Sandy being highly concentrated, the shortened hours on Monday reflect the Church's emphasis on Family Home Evening. Monday evenings are set aside for families to spend uninterrupted time together out of the busy week.

"Our winter hours are longer and our summer hours are shorter," Janel continued. "We are only open until eight in the evening in the summer. Cutting out that extra hour means a savings in salary and utility expenses. It's just smart business."

Stay consistent in your store hours, aside from making allowances for seasonal conditions. Hours that vary too much are confusing, and customers will not remember them. For instance, if you have your operating hours as Monday, Tuesday, and Thursday 9 to 4 P.M., Wednesday and Friday 9 to 2 P.M., Saturdays 10 to 4 P.M., and Sundays 11 to 4 P.M., who is going to remember all that?

Again, shop the competition and try to offer something in the way of store hours that they are not. Hobby Lobby is closed on Sundays and, believe me, Michaels in our town cleans up on that day. Weigh whether the extra hours or hour rotation is worth it to you and your stress-related workload.

SIGNAGE

I owned a sign and advertising business for many years. During that time, I argued with customers concerning their choice for color, layout, and materials, as these all affect your visibility and effectiveness.

If you are placing your store in a mall or plaza, that venue will in all likelihood dictate what type of sign you may have. Some allow neon, some do not. Backlit Plexiglas is a popular choice for many due to its visibility at night and its wide range of choices concerning vinyl lettering, logos, and color combinations for maximum impact. It is cost-effective compared to neon, and sometimes less expensive than channel letters (individual metal, plastic, or wood letters that have to have holes predrilled into the building's face or glued on).

Be careful when deciding the colors and details of your store name. What looks great on letterhead may become too cumbersome for a sign. That amazing logo of scissors, paste, and an album wasn't too costly to render on paper, but it could be astronomical to reproduce on a sign in scanned machine-cut vinyl in eight colors. Each color in a design has to be separated from the design on the computer, the correlating color of vinyl fed into a machine that then uses a blade to cut the image into the vinyl sheet. The sign artist then "weeds" the parts of the sheet that have nothing to do with the image and pulls them away, leaving only the design. A sticky transfer paper is then pressed over the image. This transfer paper with the image attached is positioned on the Plexiglas or metal sign and *squeegeed* down until the adhesive-backed vinyl is firmly in place and bubble-free. The process is repeated for each differently colored element of the design. This is time-consuming, and if the design is extremely detailed with tiny parts, the weeding can be a nightmare. This same process is used for lettering on glass windows, both on cars and on store fronts.

Keep in mind that signage is meant to be seen from a distance. Study signs as you drive by, and notice the ones that really stand out and those that you have to squint to read. The ones that usually work the best are simple but clever, and employ correct color combinations.

What is it you're offering? This may sound like a stupid question, but I have seen signs and banners where the emphasis was put on the wrong area. A case in point was a large posterboard sign being enthusiastically waved at passing traffic on a busy street corner by a group of teenagers advertising a car wash they were hosting in the adjoining parking lot. The sign read, "4-H Club Fund Raiser" in large letters. In tiny letters at the bottom of the sign, it read, "Car Wash." I had to press my face to the car window to see what it was they were selling. Having "Car Wash" as the dominant feature and *then* who was sponsoring it would have been a much smarter choice.

Are you selling "Patricia's" on your sign, or the "Scrapbooking" part? Make sure the type of business you're offering is prominent. Remember that a car going by at fifty miles an hour can only get a quick glimpse of your sign.

If you are using neon letters directly on the building face, be careful of the colors blue or purple. They take on an intense, bright hue at night that becomes fuzzy and hard to read. Ask your sign company about color choices. Don't choose colors based on the fact that your bedroom is all done hunter green. When working with advertising, color selection is very important!

Take into consideration your style of building, and try to incorporate a logo that flows with the architecture. You may move in the future, so don't let the exterior *completely* influence your choice, but give it some consideration.

Some malls and plazas offer their stores a slot on a marquee flanking the parking lot, allowing you additional advertising for traffic going by. Usually you share time slots with the other stores. They may rotate the slots every two to three months for an additional charge to you of $50 or more. Each mall has its own requirements, and you are not obligated to use the marquee if you prefer not to.

VENDORS AND DELIVERIES

Each scrapbooking store owner I interviewed listed scrapbook magazines as the number one place they looked to find manufacturers of scrapbooking merchandise.

"We order from the magazines, the Internet, and from representatives who sell us products directly," says Jeanna Maire. "We buy according to popularity, theme, and seasonal demands, as well as listening to our customers and their needs. We look at the magazines our clientele are buying to see what the market is offering."

Another huge avenue for locating vendors is trade shows and expos. Manufacturers from all over the world are there showing their merchandise and offering deals.

"The vendor will determine the method of shipping. Most use UPS, and some FedEx, and yes, larger companies are notorious for slow delivery," Jenna told me.

I heard that particular delivery feature mentioned several times. Ask the larger manufacturers to tell you up front what ETA (estimated time of arrival) to expect, and be firm about your needs, especially during the holidays and more popular wedding months.

Negotiate where you can with vendors, and always shop around. With the scrapbooking industry expanding at an alarming rate, the manufacturers will be in competition for your business more than they used to be, as more and more vendors jump on the scrapbooking bandwagon. Importers are cutting out the middleman as well and selling their wares via the Internet. You have some juggling room here.

INVENTORY

With all the pretty papers, embellishments, and new decorating ideas hitting the market weekly, it's hard not to go crazy when ordering inventory. You must be careful not to overstock or exceed your budget.

Since I'm assuming you are an avid scrapbooker yourself, you should have a handle on what the more popular decorating items and theme merchandise are. Does Disney merchandise fairly fly off the racks? Be careful of fads based on summer blockbuster movie releases that may soon fade.

Take a good look at your area and what is popular in your region. In Colorado, the lodge look is huge, and thus papers with fishing hooks and moose-antler motifs are very popular. Would that look fly in Florida? Probably not. Take into consideration the local high schools and colleges—what are their mascot colors? During graduations, these colors in your paper aisle could be big sellers. Study your area's demographics: Do you have a large population of senior citizens or a more youth-oriented market? Is your location close to a school zone where harried teachers could dash in and grab some needed objects for an art class?

Janel with The Paper Attic said that sometimes you just have to use your instincts as to what will sell and what won't. In this case her instincts were wrong and she learned a valuable lesson. "We had a vendor who kept pushing these mountain motif borders on us because we are located in Salt Lake City. They were an abstract design and kinda funky, so I was not really inspired to try them. But this guy was really persistent, so we agreed to try them on a commission basis. I put them with the other borders, not even placing them very dominantly, and they sold out the first week! I ordered more and could barely keep up with the demand. It seems the customers liked the different, trendy look they had. I now find myself more open to the unusual and artsy things people bring my way.

"It is seldom true that we are completely out of things, although the holidays can be tricky in ordering enough inventory. One year the snowmen are flying off the shelves, and the next it may be nutcrackers. We do offer rain checks if we can't get the item in time for an occasion."

Go to *www.Bizfilings.com* and *www.retailtrafficmag.com* for information on pricing inventory for retail. You will need to learn about margins (the difference in price between wholesale and retail), markups, distribution, and turnovers. These guidelines will help you price your merchandise so you make a profit even when it is discounted.

Wholesale Suppliers

Contact the vendors you've found in scrapbooking magazines and on the Internet and ask them for their wholesale prices and terms. They may have a minimum requirement for your orders; find that out now. If you can, buy directly from the manufacturer to eliminate a middleman, who will take the manufacturer's price and escalate it. Find out if they offer displays for certain products or any support materials. Do they send out flyers or newsletters alerting you to new products?

If you do find yourself dealing with a distributor, shop around for prices and shipping costs. Get a strong confirmation of delivery schedules and times.

Again, try to frequent trade shows and expos in the scrapbooking industry to meet the suppliers up close and personal and find out industry terminology and pricing patterns.

Product Orders

Know your customers and order accordingly. Obviously, the holidays are easy to calculate; other times of the year may need some ingenuity. Magazines go to print six months ahead of the holiday or seasonal times to create a demand. Study the trends.

The Home & Garden Television network has become very popular. Try and catch a few of these shows to watch growing trends, new techniques, and unique merchandising ideas. Shows such as *Martha Stewart Living* offer wonderful ideas for the scrapbooking industry.

When deciding what to order, here is a guideline: "We mainly decide what inventory to order by reviewing what's in stock," says Jeanna Maire. "Also, the computer helps us see what is moving and what is not."

The POS (point-of-sale) system we covered in chapter 3 is the most efficient way to keep track of inventory and monitor what's selling and what isn't. You can see at a glance your customers' buying patterns and use it to determine merchandise that has run its course.

MARKETING

When defining marketing, we are talking about how to get your product to move. Advertising will bring them in the door; effective marketing will get them to buy once they're inside.

"I have what I call Profit Centers," Penny McDaniel with Legacies LLC told me. "These are the different areas in the store that generate the most income. Workshops, our special photography center, albums, the papers, stamps, and embellishments. In this business you need a retail mentality, not just a scrapbooking mentality."

Pretend you're a customer just walking into your store. What do you see? Are you welcomed by a dazzling display of color and fun ideas? Does a happy employee welcome you as you enter, or are you ignored until you need help or make a purchase, at which time they are only too glad to take your money?

Your employees are a marketing tool. Train them well. They can make or break a customer's desire to return to your store.

Now that you've spent the money on product, get the most from it. If an item isn't moving, what do you do? You market it, baby. Try packaging it with another item and placing it in a visually prominent area of the store. People love bargains and getting what they perceive to be more bang for their buck. Now, instead of teddy bear paper that wasn't flying off the shelves, you have the paper and these adorable matching stickers and a bear-shaped template. You price it accordingly so that you are still making money, and now the "dead" product is being snatched up.

Penny McDaniel uses her aged items that are not moving in her classes and workshops. A wonderful idea, using the slow-moving item; suddenly the workshop attendees are scrambling to that aisle to use the product in the same manner they just saw demonstrated.

You can use the same merchandise to create idea boards. People have to be led. Show them something clever, put the means to recreate it in their hands, and they walk out happily planning their new album page.

Try moving slow merchandise around the store and displaying it in creative ways. Sometimes something just has to be repositioned to gain attention.

My favorite thing to do is brainstorm ideas. Do something fun! You have your own store, now be creative! How about Luau Days in the summertime? Group all your tropical-themed merchandise in the middle of the store beneath an inflatable palm tree you got from Party America. Have the employees wear leis and play Hawaiian music in the background. Push the travel bug feeling to urge customers to start making those vacation album pages. Make sure the Disney memorabilia is nearby. Have a drawing for a free cup of punch. Have each customer plunge her hand into a sand-filled plastic pool and pull out a small plastic shovel. On the shovel scoop, you have put a number in Magic Marker. If the number corresponds to the one you call out, they win!

Marketing is doing anything innovative and different from the competition. Keep them coming back with great ideas and outstanding customer service.

Clearance Sales

You can send out coupons in your newsletters or mailings to quickly move merchandise that is obsolete or slow in leaving the store.

"We've learned it best to discount items to try and make back at least the money we paid for them," says Jeanna Maire. "That's why sales are a win-win."

Everybody likes to feel they are getting something for nothing. Clearance sales tend to bring out the little "gimme monster" in all of us. Many people will buy things, especially crafts, thinking, "Shoot, at that price I can't go wrong . . . I'll *find* something to do with it!"

Make sure before you mark your merchandise down that you know your profit margin so that you aren't losing money.

Workshops

Workshops bring in customers and increase product sales. "I call it 'Butts in the Seats,' " grins Peggy McDaniel. "Whereas the product generates more income than the workshops, the workshops bring in customers and increase product sales."

Classes, workshops, and crops let the customers come together for a little chat time while organizing their albums and pages in a one-stop shopping environment. The work tables and chairs are there, as are supplies, merchandise, teachers, and networking. The interruptions from husband and kids are left behind.

"Crops are great for us," says Jeanna Maire of Your Crop Shop. "That's why we offer them every Saturday and Sunday from noon to midnight for only $5 per customer. They have twelve hours to shop, which they enjoy doing as they work on their personal projects.

The Paper Attic in Sandy, Utah, has six teachers who offer different scrapbooking techniques for two- to three-hour increments. "We also have a twelve-page class on Saturdays from 11 to 5 P.M. for only $25," Janel said. "We offer classes designed just for kids, teenagers, and those who just want to do basic photos without all the excess."

Think outside the album when coming up with ideas for your workshops and classes. Look at your competitors' newsletters. What can you do better? Keep an eye on events in your area that could segue into a workshop idea. Graduation, Rodeo season (yup, I'm in Colorado!). NASCAR races, weddings, the hot air balloon festival, etc.

Special Offerings

Penny McDaniel of Legacies offers an in-store photographer to scrapbookers who want to have pictures taken for their albums.

"The photographer is usually my daughter, who is a professional," Penny stated. "However, she just had my second granddaughter, so no picture-taking for her. I am also a photographer. I don't claim to be as good as my daughter, but I do some. I also have three people I contract as employees. I promote the studio, I have all the equipment and the space, and I set the appointments. It's a very unusual situation for a scrapbook store; I just chose to have it as a piece of my business plan."

"WHAT WOULD I HAVE DONE DIFFERENTLY?"

"I would have advertised that we were coming and put the signage up earlier," states Penny McDaniel of Legacies LLC. "If you don't get the word out there, they're not going to know you're here."

When asked the above question, Jeanna Maire answered, "Not much. I would have made little changes, like the flooring of the shop. We have a light-colored pretty Berber carpet; I think a laminate would be better. It's little things like that."

Other owners said they would have hired a payroll service right from the start to handle employee computation. Another was getting more space to start out with.

"A 2,500-square-foot shop just isn't big enough for this industry," Jeanna Maire said.

Others comment that they would not have used family members for employees or asked them to help with everything that had to be done to get the doors open. Family and friends often volunteer, but when it's time to show up with the buckets and mops, they suddenly have plans.

TYPICAL START-UP COSTS

Opening a new store is not inexpensive. Advertising alone (a necessity if you want people to know who and where you are) can run into the thousands. Your cost for the building will be determined by how many square feet you're leasing, upgrades, and signage.

Almost 40 percent of new stores can be opened on $10,000 or less. Another 30 percent will require start-up costs of $10,000 to $50,000. The rest average $50,000 to $100,000 or higher to get the doors open. The larger the space, the more overhead and more expense; your inventory factors in as well. Then you add employee payroll, insurance, taxes, advertising, etc. A new store could run you up to $150,000 to open your doors.

Your local commercial realtor can give you some idea of cost based on location and square footage. The landlord can show you what others who came before you have needed to set up shop.

A WORD ABOUT FRANCHISES

The scrapbooking craze is still new enough to have few franchises offered at this point. They are, however, beginning to appear on the horizon. You can type in "scrapbooking franchise opportunities" on a search engine and look for upcoming sites there. Of course, Creative Memories is the biggest franchise out there at this time if you are looking for a home-based franchise. I did find the following new venture, which may interest you:

In a 2004 article, Fun Facts Publishing (*www.funfactspublishing.com*), states statistics that show a real boom in the scrapbooking industry over the last three years, and points out that in spite of industry growth, scrapbooking retailers tend to be small and independent, thus lacking "marketing, branding, and supply-chain management expertise." Of course, one retail analyst concedes, if scrapbooking stores are to become competitive franchises, they will have to distinguish themselves from national giants in the craft industry: Michaels, Hobby Lobby, etc.

You can expect franchises in the scrapbooking industry to rise in the very near future. This leaves the door wide open for ambitious entrepreneurs who want to branch out.

CHAPTER 6

The Electric
Entrepreneur

*M*ore and more Web sites are popping up under the scrapbooking banner. As with any popular trend, entrepreneurs wet their finger and hold it to the wind to test the industry's current direction. Golfers pick a few blades of grass and toss them into the air to see which way the breeze is blowing in order to judge their next swing. If you're considering opening an Internet store, you will need a few more tricks up your sleeve than the ones mentioned above; namely, knowledge of an online business.

TODAY'S INTERNET BUSINESS

When deciding to go into business, no matter what arena, I prefer to talk to those wonderful minds that have blazed the trail before me, and hopefully tap their experience and expertise. I was lucky to enough to find one of the best in the business, and will now impart his knowledge unto you.

David Kovanen is the president of Rubber Stamp Management, the corporate offices of the "Addicted To" brands, including Addicted to Rubber Stamps and Addicted to Scrapbooking. These two Internet stores are the largest online retailers of scrapbooking and paper crafts in the world. They ship to over 167 different countries and have in stock over 250,000 products. David generously took a great deal of time in answering my questions about the Internet scrapbooking business world.

"In today's Internet business, the strong are getting stronger and the weak are getting weaker. This is true in almost every sector of retailing, and especially online sales. The majority of people don't shop online . . . so the person that can figure out how to solve that problem will be a huge success. Our great opportunity isn't stealing business from other online stores—it is in expanding the entire marketplace.

"The greatest error that most people seem to make is to think that they can compete against Wal-Mart. Many small Web sites think that they have lower overhead and therefore can sell on lower margins. They also think that people are driven solely by price. In fact, most online stamp companies tried to compete against us on price . . . and every single one of those companies failed. No discounter has succeeded against us. Not one. That should say something. The companies that succeed are those that sell value, not discounters."

Today's Internet market is bursting at the seams. This has its upside and its downside, obviously. Can you cash in on this booming online industry? Certainly. Will it take some ingenuity and building a better mousetrap? Yep. Is there room for one more store? Yes, but, you need to really do your research in this area.

Cyberspace has become the one-stop shopping mecca of this generation. Look at the benefits involved:

Benefits of Running an Internet Business

You can set up shop anywhere, and your customers will never see your working environment. If you want to do business in your bathrobe while sipping a latte and listening to Beethoven, you can. You can work on your Web site at midnight or 5 A.M., hours most businesses aren't open. With a dazzling Web site, you can rival the competition even though you may live in humble surroundings. Your customer base is now millions of people looking at your site, instead of a dozen or more who might wander into a brick-and-mortar setup.

The benefits to your customers are huge as well. They can shop your store 24/7 in the comfort of *their* homes in *their* pajamas. Comparison shopping takes a matter of minutes rather than the hours a trip to multiple stores in your city would take. Shipment is quick, it comes right to their door, or they can have it shipped to a friend as an instant gift—not too shabby.

Realistically, you need to look at how great the competition is and stick your toe in the water to determine the temperature before you dive in. If you enter "scrapbooking stores" in a search engine such as Google, you will come up with 20,300 hits as of this printing. Research these sites and get a feel for what you will be up against, then determine whether you can offer something better.

DESIGNING A WEB SITE

You have many options here when it comes to creating a Web site. Stores such as Best Buy and Circuit City offer software at an inexpensive price that allows you to build one step by step. You can hire a professional and pay anywhere from $280 to upwards of $1,000 or more for a professional site with all the bells and whistles. Asking Cousin Mert with his computer technology to build you one is an option. I would advise creating your own. A simple class or some of the online tutorials can help you come up with an eye-catching, customer-friendly Internet store. Libraries offer books on Web design, too.

I'm an advocate of doing things yourself if you possibly can. For instance, if you design your own Web site, you will know how to troubleshoot it or add new features instead of waiting for your Webmaster to get around to it and charging you for his time. You'll be adding and deleting features constantly, so why not have the skills and knowledge at your fingertips?

There are many Web hosts that provide on-site setups with simple formats that you can use for a basic site. Go to *www.comparewebhosts.com* and research the different options. "The simplest way is to set up a store on Yahoo!. That's what I would do if I were starting a small online company," states David Kovanen.

Compare other sites and jot down what you like and don't like about them. Start with the basics: How's the layout? Is it confusing or too busy? How do they group their merchandise, and are the prices clearly visible? What color themes are they using? Never underestimate good marketing tricks such as color and layout. I have skipped over many a site because it simply did not appeal to me visually.

Now, with your list of preferences, begin to design your own. If you were a customer, what would you want in a Web site to make your shopping, easy, fun, and informative? Make sure your Web site is easy to navigate. Nothing is more frustrating than being kicked off a site or moved around in circles because the setup has not been professionally done. Always check your Web site yourself periodically to make sure the connections, shopping cart, credit card setup, etc. are working and easy to use. I recently had a page where the e-mail link was not working. You can lose valuable customers over small glitches like this.

Most sites offer free layout ideas and decorating packages; some have chat rooms and networking setups. What can you offer that the others don't?

HOW TO STAND OUT FROM THE CROWD

David Kovanen of Rubber Stamp Management says, "We battle this every day. How can *we* stand out? Our strategy is simple: Earn your reputation on every single order and every single day. We have taken ten years to build a reputation, slowly. It's just hard. I don't have a lot of advice for others. Every company needs to find its own niche. What you cannot be is a copy of another company. So, you need to find something important that is totally different and unique and that you can build your reputation on.

"One company did elude us and developed a niche while we weren't looking. In five years they have grown to be nearly our size in scrapbooking . . . but in a unique combination of home sales and online sales. We're in a catch-up situation. We'll probably spend several hundred thousand dollars recapturing our share of that niche. But this is all proof that niches are out there and are viable."

Getting your URL (Universal Resource Locator), a fancy name for your domain name or Internet address, on major search engines such as Yahoo! and Ask Jeeves is a must. One way to try to get your business listed is to log on to *www.submitexpress.com*. This Web site will get your information to over forty search engines. Make sure you list your store on Web sites that list Internet scrapbook stores such as Jangle (*www.jangle.com*) and Scraplink (*www.scraplink.com*). Hit the scrapbook chat rooms, newsgroups, and any other avenue that will keep you in touch with scrappers and their interests and needs, in order to learn what might help you better differentiate your site.

The best way to stand out from the competition is to do your homework and really research what others are doing online. Make a list of your competitors and list what they are doing well and what could be better. How many offer shopping carts, contests, message boards, or chats?

REGISTERING YOUR DOMAIN NAME

Your domain name, or URL, should identify your business, such as *www.scrapbookworld.com*. You will need to scout an Internet registry to see if your name is already taken. As with signage, don't try to "tweak" it if someone else has already accessed that name. Adding a word of two to make it yours will only confuse your customers, and your competitor may receive some of your business. For instance, if you want *www.Albums&Ancestors.com* and someone already has that name, don't be tempted to call yours *www.Ancestors&Albums.com*.

Use a search engine and type in "domain registry" to check for the availability of your chosen URL. The registration fees will vary, so shop around. Some are as little as $20 annually. "*GoDaddy.com* is reasonably priced, and their service is outstanding," according to David Kovanen.

WHO'S YOUR HOST?

In the Internet world, a host is the place where your online store will be found. The number of hosts is more prolific than muffins at a Martha Stewart bake-off, so shop around. There will be a monthly fee involved and services vary, so research them carefully. These hosts will provide you with your own domain name, good service, reliable tech support, and preferably enough online space for your growing needs.

The Yahoo! Store comes highly recommended by several experts in the field. If all this Internet terminology is confusing, go to *www.thefreedictionary.com* or *www.URLdefinition.com* to learn the lingo.

CREDIT CARD SETUP

We've already discussed the enormous amount of plastic shopping going on. Eighty percent of online shoppers use credit cards. You will lose sales if you do not have this amenity. Therefore, you should buy software from merchant account providers and vendors who charge a processing fee and installation fee for each purchase. This is not unlike the retail merchant's arrangement with credit card companies. This software also allows your customers the convenience of entering their credit card data once instead of typing it each time a transaction is made.

David Kovanen says, "The Yahoo! Store takes care of the credit card problem. Otherwise, the credit card problem is always difficult. We do millions of dollars a year in credit card sales . . . and they are still just as difficult to work with as when we were small. There is no good answer. And, while you can sign up for Visa and MasterCard in one application, you must sign up for AmEx and Discover separately."

PayPal is a great credit card service offered to customers who want the security of offering their credit card information once and paying only one service. When you pay PayPal, PayPal credits you electronically. See *www.paypal.com* for information. It is a boon to eBay shoppers and heavily used.

NEED A CART?

The idea is to make your site one-stop shopping, so if you are inclined to, load it with all the conveniences. Give your customers a "cart" to push around and load up while visiting your online store. Each of the purchases they click on is added to a list and tallied, complete with shipping charges. Checking out of your store is easy and quick.

AUCTIONS

eBay has put online auctioning on the map. The enormous popularity of being able to spotlight a product and have millions of shoppers bid on it is astronomical. In the scrapbooking industry, scrappers are putting their items up for bid on such sites as *www.twopeasinabucket.com* and *www.ebay.com*. The Yahoo! Site, *www.groups.yahoo.com*, hosts auctions such as Scrapswap and Trading Everything.

MESSAGE BOARDS

A message board at your store site is a glorified bulletin board in the teacher's lounge, but worth the time it takes to create and monitor it. Visitors to your site can post questions, offer insight, advice, and creative ideas, etc. The site *www.message-boards.net* will get you started in creating this customer service tool.

"If I could do things over, we would have a strong message board," says David Kovanen, "but we don't, and it would be quite difficult to establish one."

David recommends that you monitor the board constantly to watch for information from outside sources that could damage your business. Remember, your customers will assume that if the information is on your message board, then you must condone it.

E-MAIL

Since I am a huge advocate of outstanding customer service, let me recommend adding a "Contact Us" feature to your store. Allow customers the opportunity to ask questions or voice complaints like they would at a retail brick-and-mortar store. E-mailing your clientele with upcoming sales and promotions is also important.

David Kovanen puts it this way: "E-mail is important. But you need to do it. The problem is that every year it's less and less effective, because of spammers.

If spam could be eliminated, e-mail would be more effective. We have over 80,000 names in our e-mail list, and we know that the list helps us.

"Also, e-mail is important for customer service. Nothing will ruin a business faster that to take more than one business day to respond to messages. We try to respond within four hours, and that is longer than we would like. E-mail consumes *gobs* of time, so you have to manage that. Use a lot of personal but canned answers; if you don't, you will find yourself spending fifteen minutes on every inquiry. Since your time is money, you can find you are spending $10 for every e-mail you take time to answer. The secret is to be prompt and timely, but not spend too much time on any one message."

CHAT ROOMS

You can offer chat room facilities at your store for customers to chat with others about various scrapbooking topics. Having a scheduled guest speaker or theme is a great idea to bring people to your site to have an interactive conversation with an expert in a certain area of scrapbooking.

Be careful with chat rooms, however, as they can get away from you. Some chats become combative, and it could reflect on your store. If you can't monitor the chat, it may be best to skip this and stay with a message board.

AFFILIATE PROGRAMS

The old "you scratch my back and I'll scratch yours" rule applies to affiliate programs. Basically, you offer to sell books that would interest your customer market from Amazon (*www.amazon.com*), Barnes & Noble (*www.bn.com*), etc. You place the book cover graphic, price, and description on your site, and if a customer clicks on it, she is put in touch with your affiliate sponsor, such as Amazon. Amazon now pays you a 15 percent commission for selling the book *for* them. There are some wonderful deals out there and software to help you keep track of the transactions; check out *www.affiliatezone.com* for all your needs in this area.

WAVE YOUR BANNER

Banner ads will either generate a growl or a smile, depending on whom you talk to. They are those blinking boxes at the top of Web sites designed to catch your attention.

"Banners were once a cost-effective way of advertising," according to David Kovanen, "but today we find that they are not. (We did no banner advertising in 2004.) Above all else, use tracking codes in your banner ads. Unless you track the cost-effectiveness of your banner ads, you will be wasting your money. You should absolutely be able to measure how many sales you get from each banner ad. Look at what percentage of sales the banner ads are costing you. If you cannot measure the effectiveness, then do not do them. It's just that simple.

"Also, a simple change of banner can up its effectiveness by a factor of five. (I'm not kidding!) Just changing a background color can alter the effectiveness. So, run several banner ads and measure the response. You will be surprised. The ad you like best will probably do the worst. I cannot predict which ad will work best, so we measure every one and let our customers decide. Absolutely monitor your banners with a click-through rate to equate the cost of the banner ad to the revenues it generates. If you don't do that, you will waste your money. Remember, you are designing the banner ads to generate sales, not creating museum art. Do what works."

TAXING QUESTIONS

Internet retailers are not required to collect sales tax, which has retail store fronts and home-based businesses up in arms. This is just one more advantage, and an unfair one, retailers and local and state government scream about the Internet industry. The loss of revenue is keenly felt. With the cry and hue over this touchy area, it is my guess that Congress will pass a law in the near future taxing Internet sales.

PACKAGING

Packaging materials can be a tricky part of the online business when shipping orders out to customers.

"We went several years before we developed our own perfect packaging," says David Kovanen. "We used bubbles and peanuts and butcher paper and probably everything else you can imagine. In our unusual case, we ended up using custom-designed boxes and custom materials. Even the tape on the boxes is custom-manufactured because we cannot get good enough quality off the shelf.

"Dunnage, the stuff that fills a void inside a box (like peanuts and bubble pack), is surprisingly expensive. It costs about $2 per cubic foot—an expense many people forget. So, start by recycling incoming materials, although you will never have enough. You just can't be adding $2 an order in packing materials . . . but I see many online companies doing exactly that.

"Also, don't buy the cheapie boxes. They will crush, they will 'dribble' products out the corners, and they will not protect packages. This is the reason that we (and all large shippers) use quality boxes. You cannot imagine the abuse that a product receives while being shipped!

"Consider breakage: One ink refill that breaks open can ruin a $50 order. And the customer will expect you to replace the entire order. So, beware of which products can leak and package them specially.

"Consider chaffing: Products that touch each other can wrinkle or chafe. Customers will demand replacement products when this happens. We used to paper-clip the invoice to products in the package. The paper clip would leave a small mark and customers would demand replacements. So, consider even the little details.

"And, use a tracking number. Certain customers out there will look to see if you tracked the package. And, if the package arrives without a tracking number, they will wait a couple of weeks and then claim that it never arrived. They are very good at this game, and they are very insistent. You will constantly have to send them replacement orders until you learn to track the packages. We estimate 3 percent of all orders will get 'lost' if you do not use a tracking number—sad, but true. Track everything and keep the records of every package.

"We digitally photograph every order being shipped. You just cannot keep enough documentation."

The Internet scrapbooking store is a temptation that should be carefully looked over.

"It's a nice home business that you can get into inexpensively, and you don't have to work retail hours (evenings and weekends), and some customers are genuinely fun to work with," states Kovanen. "The cons are that it is a lot more work than it looks like, and there is a lot more competition nationwide than you can imagine. So, you may not experience the success you envisioned. National advertising is expensive, and the existing companies are pretty good at what they do.

"If you do find the right niche product, you can be quite successful. One five-year-old start-up that found a niche that we couldn't address is now a $3 million to $3.5 million a year business!"

CHAPTER 7

Designing Your Own Products

With the exploding scrapbooking industries churning up the waters of profitability, it's only natural that a boatload of new products would follow in its wake. As more men and women discovered the delight of creating albums and foraged through stores for more and more unique and time-saving implements, ideas began to grow. "What if this template offered more than one shape?" "Could I play up the snowman-themed paper by adding faux snow-flocked cutouts?"

With these questions came the age-old question, "Great idea . . . now what?" You have the idea brightly burning, now what's the first step to bring it to fruition? Don't stop now! With some, the light's wattage increases as they set out to put their brainchild into action; with others, the bulb dims and eventually extinguishes. It can seem like a daunting process indeed to get from Idea A to Product Sales B.

My family and I love going to the movie theatre. I'll admit there are few new releases we have not attended if the content was inappropriate. During my frequent concession-stand runs, I got into the habit of buying popcorn and chocolate-covered Raisinettes. My thing was to put a handful of popcorn in my mouth and then add some Raisinettes at the same time, so that I had chocolate and popcorn going at the same time. My family teased me endlessly about this fetish, but I continued happily on. It was delicious! I told friends about it, and they laughed as well.

Three months ago, guess what hit the stores? Blockbuster and other movie outlets are now offering the newest thing on the market. Microwave popcorn with a bag of Raisinettes added, to be sprinkled over the freshly popped kernels. My idea is now cleaning up in stores! Every time I see the combo offered on the shelves, I moan. Next time, I will forget the snickers I get from my family and peers and head for the closest patent search information center.

FINDING A MARKET

Your first step is to find out if there is a need for that idea that woke you up the last five nights at three in the morning. You just know it will be revolutionary and every scrapper out there will want one . . . or two . . . or a fleet-full! But before you spend money on patent searches, prototypes, and advertising, you need to determine whether there really is a need, or if you are just caught up in the excitement of the moment.

Obviously, your target market will be other scrappers. How do you get their feedback on your great new tool without risking them stealing your idea? It's tricky, but it can be done.

Try to wrangle an invitation to a crop meet or similar scrapbooking workshop. Turn the conversation to the area your idea centers around. For instance, if you've come up with an idea for a baby-themed paper with die-cut slits for album creators to slide a picture of a newborn into a slot atop a printed rocking horse, then say something like this: "Wow, there are so many papers geared to babies, aren't there?"

You will get a number of responses, from a muffled assent to, "I know . . . it's nuts!" You walk quietly around the table, peering over heads at their handiwork, and casually toss out, "They're all kind of generic, though, don't you think? You know, all baby ducks and sailboats and rattles." Again, you will get varied responses.

You add, "If someone came up with an innovative way to attach baby pictures to a nursery-themed paper that was witty and different, would you buy it?"

Listen to the responses; really listen. These are your future customers. They may let some pearls of wisdom drop that you hadn't thought of. One may even inadvertently blurt out that she saw a nursery-themed paper in the scrapbook store with slits in it for baby picture placement.

Before you go slam the car door on your foot in a fit of rage and disappointment, realize that this woman just saved you a lot of time and expense. Which brings me to my next point: Do your research! Don't peek down a few aisles at the only two scrapbook stores in your city and say, "Nope . . . don't see anything like my idea," and clap your hands and head for the nearest attorney. Get on the Internet and scout out the megastores, call retail outlets outside your immediate area, and check magazines geared to scrapbook merchandise.

PATENT SEARCH

You can hire an attorney to do a patent search for you, join an Internet one-stop shopping product development agency such as Invention Home, or do it yourself. An attorney can charge hundreds of dollars to run this search for you. Attorneys will charge anywhere from $5,000 to $15,000 for a full utility patent once you've decided to procure one. One such Web site attorney specializing in patents is Michael Neustel, a U.S. registered patent attorney. He offers advice on patents, trademarks, copyrights, and marketing. You can find him at the Neustel Law Offices at *www.patentapplications.com*.

Internet patent companies will do the search for you and some throw in other benefits as well. The best one I found is Invention Home, which literally does it all. I spoke in length with Russell Williams from Jacob Entertainment and Invention Home. They have revolutionized the entire product development market. For one price, you can have them do a patent search, build a virtual reality prototype of your design in 3-D, gain access to their network of manufacturers who are looking for new ideas, post your resume and Web site, and offer an online invention tradeshow, similar to Monster.com for job searchers. Companies come to the trade show looking for new ideas to market. You are protected by a nondisclosure form, and they offer you a provisional patent for one year. Thus, instead of spending upwards of $50,000 to have an attorney, graphic designer, marketing agent, etc., do all of these steps, you can be spotlighted to over 500 manufacturers for less than $3,000 for a 3-D virtual reality site. The price is reduced if you prefer to have 2-D or a simplified program. They even offer you availability to their team of lawyers at reduced fees. Russell is very proud of this groundbreaking program, as well he should be.

The third option is to do it yourself. The U.S. Trade and Patent Office's database is at *www.uspto.gov*. They also offer an automated information line at (800) PTO-9199. You can type "patent search" into a search engine and find other avenues there. Some are geared specifically to certain areas such as technological or biological patents, so research the offers carefully.

MAKING A PROTOTYPE

Whatever your new idea is, you will need to build some type of design to show to manufacturers in order to gauge their enthusiasm and obtain orders. This design is called a *prototype*. It can be as simple as a new background paper that you've made yourself using artist's paints and card stock, or as elaborate as a metal or plastic template you hired someone to cut for you with specialized machinery.

A prototype shows your prospective buyers exactly what you are offering, its degree of complexity, an idea of the costs to manufacture it, and its possible appeal to the target market. It may be a design they would be willing to purchase from you outright for a one-time fee, or they could negotiate a possible royalty setup. They may offer to cover the manufacturing costs and advertising in exchange for you receiving a smaller cut of the profit pie.

If you are serious enough to go to the trouble of making a prototype, make it a good one. Don't think you can show up with a cardboard circle you cut from the underside of a shoebox and gain support and enthusiasm from busy executives who deal with professional businessmen who have laid a well thought out and expensively made design before them on their polished cherrywood conference table. Be prepared to lay out some money up front, whether it is to have a graphic artist create your design using the latest in computer software or to hire a machinist with die-cut tool capabilities.

I mentioned previously in this chapter what a boon virtual prototypes are to the invention industry. Now, instead of hand-creating your masterpiece or paying someone else to do so, your interested party can simply click on a Web site and have your brainchild vividly displayed before him in full color and animated brilliance. Rendered in 3-D graphics, your prototype image will rotate and show every angle and advantage. The summary of its benefits will be listed prominently and your contact information displayed. Instead of peddling your little box of goodies to a few manufacturers a week, you are now represented before hundreds in a day. Russ gave me this quote right before this book went to press:

❦ ❦ ❦ ❦ ❦ ❦ ❦ ❦ ❦ ❦ ❦ ❦ ❦ ❦ ❦ ❦ ❦ ❦ ❦

"In my view, with our patented marketing method, we have
the strongest marketing network in the invention industry. We have
the approach and means for pulling the invention information
together (via Web sites and virtual technology), and most importantly,
the ability to easily communicate the information to our
networks of agents, manufacturers, and distributors.

"We also recently signed an agreement with an international trading company to provide our inventors, distributors, and agents with low-cost overseas manufacturing (very low China pricing), which means we can not only supply a distributor with new product lines, but we can also connect them with the low manufacturing costs—very powerful."

❧ ❦ ❧ ❦ ❧ ❦ ❧ ❦ ❧ ❦ ❧ ❦ ❧ ❦ ❧ ❦ ❧ ❦ ❧ ❦

For further information, contact Russ Williams at *rwilliams@invention-home.com*.

Whenever you are presenting your design to anyone, whether it be the artist you've hired to create the prototype or the manufacturer you show it to, always have them sign a nondisclosure form assuring you that they will not steal your idea and run with it. Make detailed notes of your correspondence with them; have them initial any sketches you've made and date them. Cover yourself at every step.

PRICING

If you are marketing your own products, rather than licensing the design or selling it outright, the price you decide on when you first put your product on the market is the one you'll be working with for the entirety of its lifespan. You cannot escalate your price down the road. If your starting price isn't high enough, your margin could hit zero before you know it. As the product gets lower on the retail chain, so does your price. It may start out in a prominent position on Aisle 2 of a scrapbooking store franchise at $3.50 and end up at $0.75 in the clearance bin a few months later. Remember that no matter how you wish to price your item, you must also consider what the retailer's profit needs are, as well as what the market will bear.

"I have bought from a couple of locals who made their own products," Penny McDaniel of Legacies told me. "One of them was on consignment (cards) and I just paid her with store credit. Unfortunately, she thought we should charge x amount of dollars for them, which meant there was no way to put the normal markup on them—they would just be too expensive for our clients. Needless to say, I didn't sell many, and only left them out for about six weeks. I thought that was plenty of time to try it.

"The other local had die-cuts of the local high schools—which was great. I agreed I would pay her upon delivery, but when she delivered them to me, I saw they were not packaged at all. I was able to sell some based on product demand, but it wasn't professional or easy for me. Now I have a lot left over. I hope they want them next May again!"

What it costs you make an item (or have it made for you) is only one factor in deciding what price to charge, and is by no means determinative. Calculating the cost of the plastic or metal or paper and other raw materials is not hard. It's the peripherals that are tough. Say you start out marketing on the East Coast, get a lot of publicity, and begin to realize a nationwide market. Now you're also selling on the West Coast, and transportation becomes a large element in your costs . . . one you never factored in.

Many beginners figure, "Oh, I'll just mark it up 50 percent, and that should cover any unexpected things that come up." It might; it might not. There's a lot to be considered besides the cost of producing the product: delivery charges, promotion, invoicing, paperwork, deadbeats, and so on. There are phone calls and mailing expenses, gas and oil as you drive your idea around locally, and airfare to trade shows. Price your idea for as much as the market will allow. The typical pricing markup is 50 percent in this industry, but you must consider your overhead individually.

What happens if you hit it big? Selling a thousand units to a few local stores is one thing; selling 50,000 implies extra costs: transportation, sales commission, returns, collection problems, and paperwork. If you've been making these decorations at home, and selling 50 or 60 a week, and you suddenly get a big order for 50,000, you will probably have to outsource the work. Having your invention manufactured may actually be cheaper per unit than making it at home yourself, but the start-up costs involved can be prohibitive. Like I said, you can't bump the price up later without it hurting you. Make the price work to start with.

A final word on pricing: Beware of the "knock-off" potential. If you have a particularly great idea and it is moving well, others will be only too happy to make a few modifications, package it in a more eye-catching container, and try to undersell you to boot. What will that do to your profit margin? Again, price it right to start with.

COPYRIGHTS

You can copyright just about anything—a book, song, dance, design, sketch, any tangible object. You cannot copyright an idea, however. You can only copyright the wording or formation of the idea. If someone takes what I've written and reproduces it verbatim without my permission, he is liable for legal action. That little "©" carries a lot of weight.

A copyright can be had without registering it. I can simply name a product and type "Annie Richmond, Copyright 2004," and I have a copyright. But should the time come to enforce it, I would be better off if I had registered it. By registering, you let the world know when you came up with your design and exactly what it is. The document filed at the Copyright Office is proof and will stand up in a court of law.

You can register your copyright by calling the Library of Congress in Washington, D.C., at (202) 707–5000 and asking for an application. Fill it out and send off two copies of what you want to have copyrighted (plus two models if it is a design), along with $30, to the Library of Congress, 101 Independence Ave. S.E, Washington, D.C. 20559–6000. You now have a copyright good for your lifetime plus seventy years. Your best bet, however, is probably to go the Web site of the Copyright Office, *www.copyright.gov*, because there you will be able to read about updates and changes to the law, download various copyright forms for ideas fixed in different media, and receive information about how to fill out forms and how to file.

Another avenue is via the Web sites offered by different businesses who will do all the work for you. Robert Shapiro, noted attorney to O.J. Simpson, among others, has co-founded LegalZoom.com (*www.legalzoom.com*), a site dedicated to handling most legal complexities involved in copyright. The company will create a federal application for $119. The U.S. government application fee is another $30 on top of that. LegalZoom.com will file the copyright application with the U.S. Copyright Office for free.

Another such Web site is *www.copyrightassistant.com*, which will register your copyright for $89.99. Check around and look closely at what these companies offer.

TRADEMARK

A trademark identifies or distinguishes a product or brand from all other products out there in scrapbook land. Trademarks such as Coca-Cola and Xerox are industry giants and have become synonymous with their products. Most attorneys will charge you close to $700 to create and file a trademark application. With this, you can register your trademark and let the world know this mark is yours. No one can come in later and claim rights to your product.

If you are interested in registering your trademark, you should go to the Web site of the United States Patent and Trademark Office, *www.uspto.gov.* The information on this site will tell you how to go through the steps of obtaining the trademark—the first thing you will need to do is to search, or hire someone to search, to make sure the trademark isn't already owned—and lead you through electronic registration of a trademark.

Again, you may also want to consider the Web sites offering to help you with your trademark procurement. LegalZoom.com will register a U.S. trademark for $149; this includes a free *basic* search. The federal filing fee is an additional $335. They will do a *comprehensive* trademark search for $199 (please see the site for details). For an additional $175, they will conduct detailed periodic searches to alert you if any similar trademarks are filed or published.

PACKAGING

As an advertiser and graphic artist, I realize the importance of great packaging. Take book covers, for instance. The title alone can sell a book even though books on the same topic and written better are setting right next to it. You have to grab people's imagination. In chapter 10, Advertising, we will cover the power of creative marketing in full. For now, let's consider your package design.

If a marketer set a creatively designed cereal box next to a bland, "brown paper bag"–looking container, which do you think you or your child would select? I don't care if the full-color box housed two scoops of five-day-old bread crumbs—the impetus to reach for the attractive box would be high. Advertising agencies are paid big bucks to make their client's product stand out on a shelf where consumers are quickly perusing items to make a purchase. Let me tell you, this is an involved procedure. We are talking psychology and color theory here; everything to push that shopper's hand in the direction manufacturers want it to go.

Now let's look at your product. If it's a creative paper, you don't have a package per say; the paper *is* the package. It's right out there for all to see and evaluate, with perhaps a bar code and price sticker on its back. You will have to depend on the gorgeous background you created to make it sell. There are other scrapbook items that don't necessarily come in packages, such as rubber stamps, metal plaques, fancy pens, etc. That doesn't mean you can't do something clever with the colors or the name. What would make *you* pick up that item if a similar one were hanging next to it?

If you do have an item that can be bagged, boxed, or pressure sealed, how can you design it to make an impact? I'm a firm believer in humor. Make the customer smile, and you've got him. Come up with a clever tag board attached to your plastic sleeve for your "widgets." If you are selling moose-shaped templates, how about "Just Moosin' Around"? Choose colors that "pop" and keep it simple.

Remember, those wonderful ideas to create elaborate packaging that will set your product apart from the crowd add up in cost. You have a fine line here. Each color you choose will cost an additional setup fee at the printer's. You can't just pick out twelve colors because they look great together; those colors will add up to a fortune. Can you think of a creative way to package it without incurring the cost? Yes, folks . . . that's why we pay the advertising geniuses; this is what they do for a living, and they agonize over it every day of their lives.

Study the merchandise at the scrapbooking stores. What catches your eye? Why does it? The color combination or the cute choice of words? An unusual die-cut shape in the tag hanger or a clever new way to use a see-through plastic? You cannot underestimate the power of great packaging. It can boost your sales or sink you.

"This industry is one of the worst for marketing products," Penny McDaniel told me. "You would think that they would be wonderfully creative! No. I often repackage. I rarely get a POP (point-of-purchase) display from vendors, which in any other industry is common to try to get the most focus in a store. Plus, it's a value add for a small independent trying to get some help, but not in this industry! I hope they change their ways soon!"

I noticed while researching stores that the use of color in the packaging and cardboard tags was a huge eye-catcher. Large, unique type fonts were another plus. Generic, boring, blasé colors and type only get lost. The competition between products in these stores is tremendous, and packaging is everything. Clever graphics are wonderful. I picked up a package of reindeer cutouts where there was a large goofy-eyed deer on the tag with bulging eyes. He made me laugh, and I brought him home.

THE ART OF SALES

The most effective way to get your product before the consumer, manufacturer, or retail store owner is to buy a booth at a scrapbooking trade show or expo. Depending on the size of the show, a booth could run you anywhere from $150 to $1,000. The amount of floor space and number of tables you require will also determine the cost, as will your electrical needs, partitions, and hardware (hooks for banners, clips, etc.). Most shows require that you join their trade organization, register, have a resale tax number, show a valid business license, and present other business identification documents to qualify for admission.

Many of these shows are conducted worldwide and attended by representatives from around the globe and well worth the money to set your new idea in motion. As with the packaging of the product, you cannot overlook the importance of a "knock 'em dead" booth setup. These people are often streaming by in an effort to see all of the booths and single out their favorites. Your booth has to grab them from the flow and plant them firmly before your product. One tested method is to be standing before your booth and offering a drawing or a free handout with your advertising on it. I personally get tired of stopping every few feet to fill out a drawing card, but I'm always available for a freebie gift.

Think outside the booth. Do something the others aren't doing. Would a cute costume on your unwilling ten-year-old make people stop and smile? Would a demonstration of your product in use make curious shoppers pause? Music, balloons, spin the wheel of prizes, a riddle contest. Men are a sucker for contests involving sports skills. Place a putting mat in front of your booth and offer a giveaway for anyone sinking one putt out of three. Remember, a good many retailers and manufacturers will be men— don't make it too cutesy.

Most scrapbook magazines such as *Memory Makers* will list upcoming trade shows and expos in their pages. Large Web sites dedicated to the scrapbook industry, such as (*www.scrapbook.com*), are always offering information on the latest shows and trends. Also check out the HIA (Hobby Industry Association) and ACCI (Association of Crafts and Creative Industries) Web sites. Memory Trends by *Craftrends Magazine* is another source to type into your Google.

Take your creation directly to retailers and sell your wares. A good many locally owned stores will buy your product if the price is right and they like it. Franchises and chains will require you to go to the head of the company for the final decision. Your professionalism, dress, and enthusiasm count big time here. If you're not excited about it, why should they be? Do something clever. Don't just plop your product on the counter and say, "Whatcha think?" If you are selling a clever apple sticker for teachers, place the plastic bag of stickers in a country basket filled with fake grass from a party store or from shredded crepe paper. Heck, stick a stuffed toy dog resembling Toto in there too, if it will make them smile. Market yourself! No one else will. Besides, your clever idea of using the basket sparks their marketing ideas on how to sell your product.

Another avenue is *Scrapbook Premier*, a product publication that goes out to scrapbook retail stores in the United States, showing the latest merchandise in this industry. Their phone number is (435) 586-1449. To make local sales, frequent craft sales, crops, and direct mail marketing, and leave brochures in prominent places like libraries.

CHAPTER 8

Teacher, Consultant, and Commissioned

he ability to teach something you love is a joy indeed. You take others by the hand who are eager to travel the path you have traveled, and show them the wonders of scrapbooking, with all its newest embellishments and themes. Being commissioned to create something for others is also a fantastic way to make money; you are using your skills and improving someone's life at the same time. There are few avenues for income as filled with nostalgia and sentiment as making a profit with scrapbooking. You are dealing with the client's memories and a desire to leave a legacy for her family. The fact that clients are entrusting you with such an important task should not be taken lightly.

TEACHING CLASSES FROM HOME

We've covered the pros and cons of running a business from your home in chapter 4. Here we will concentrate on teaching classes, not just selling product.

First of all, you have to be able to stand before a group of people and be calm and enthusiastic. If you get clammy hands at the thought of teaching a class, you may want to either reconsider teaching or take classes in subjects like speech, oration, or joining your local Toastmasters club to learn to appear before a group in a professional and easy manner. It won't matter if you are the foremost authority on scrapbook techniques; if you can't engage your audience and help them to have a good time and be happy they came, they won't likely return. A fantastic teacher always has an impact on students—you remember the outstanding ones from your school days, and so do I. They had the qualities of a true love for their topic, a genuine concern for their students' learning, and usually a terrific personality or gentle compassion.

If you feel you are a "people" person and think you can create an environment of fun and learning, then next you must decide just what type of classes you wish to teach.

The setup for your workshops will need careful consideration. If yours is a home-based business, you must insure that classes are free from interruption from family members and pets. One thing that has always concerned me is the inconsiderateness pet owners sometime show to visiting guests. Their love of Fido blinds them to the fact that he is licking a poor woman's leg or drooling on her purse. When it comes to business, this is magnified. Keep the pets and kids from the area.

Do you have more than adequate lighting? You are working with detailed pieces of album decoration, and eyestrain will drain your class of its enthusiasm. Is there elbow room and a nearby washroom? How is the ventilation? Are the needed supplies ready and organized in nearby display cases or shelves? If you're offering refreshments, is your carpet "punch-friendly"? A separate entrance to the work area would be a great asset. If you are teaching on a regular basis, you may wish to consult the local fire department to make sure you are in compliance with entrance and exit regulations.

Choose Your Strong Topics

Some clients may just want the basics. They want their pictures out of the box and onto an organized page—period. No fluff or hours of embellishments. You can offer a class on the basics, including page layout, grouping pictures by theme, date, or person, etc. It's amazing how many people are afraid to begin. They look at boxes overflowing with photos and think, "Where do I start?" That's where you come in. You may have to hold their hand and start with having them sort the pictures into some order before even picking up a glue stick.

Introduction to Scrapbooking

With all the new merchandise appearing daily on the shelves of retail scrapbook stores, it's no wonder many new scrappers feel overwhelmed. "What does this doohickey do? Am I supposed to draw inside this, or around it?"

Offer a class on the basics. Teach them words such as "lignan-free," "webhinge," and "die-cut." Show the advantages of certain tools over others and the best paper products to buy. What about color theory? Putting complementary colors together is more than mere guesswork; it's a science. Why does a night sky paper in purple look great with gold stars? Because yellow is across the color wheel from purple and thus is its complementary color. The same applies to blue and orange, and red and green. Yes, you guessed it . . . Christmas is perfectly color coordinated.

Offer workshops that teach how to match borders with papers and then add elements of décor such as brads, ribbons, and punches. What about page layouts? This is an area that is based on concepts of balance, scale, and proportion. Some scrappers wonder why their pages look cluttered and busy while another scrapper, using the same materials, has an album page that is a pleasure to look at because she understood the concept of employing negative space as well as positive space.

Teach the rewards of journaling. Today's albums are not just a collection of pictures, but have the written word penned in beautiful handwriting next to them, commemorating the moment. A class on calligraphy might be a great additional workshop to offer.

I've been asked to teach journaling and calligraphy to classes in scrapbooking and other craft lines. Calligraphy is a beautiful art and adds so much to a page. To see something written in a flowing scroll is so much more dramatic and creative than the typewritten word. While there are calligraphy kits in many craft stores, people are often intimidated by the seeming perfection of the script, and they appreciate having a teacher to hold their hands and encourage them.

Specialize

Now add classes that focus on particular techniques, such as rubber stamping, embossing, photo tints, use of specialty templates, punch art, brads, tags, and borders.

Show scrappers how to save time by teaching the correct way new merchandise can be used and innovative ways the manufacturer may not even have considered. Read current scrapbook magazines religiously, noting new products and trends. Bring to your classes the latest and best, thus always keeping their interest. Have different skill levels of workshops for beginners, advanced, and experts. Some of the newer techniques, such as quilted pages and specialty folded papers, may be a little advanced and confusing to a beginner.

Penny McDaniel of Legacies gave her views on the use of class materials: "We are always trying to be creative—it's the nature of the business! Creative on Demand is my new line in the store. We have done lots, but any time we make a sample using the products, those products fly off the shelf, and then we have to take the sample down because our customers get mad that we don't have the stuff in."

What's in a Theme?

Theme albums are big business—holidays, weddings, baby books, vacation, sports, commemorative albums for retirement and achievements, etc. Offer workshops based on specific and coordinated themes. There is no idea that cannot be expounded on in pages of tastefully rendered art and photos. Think outside the page, so to speak. You could help students come up with their own unusual, but touching, specialty albums. What about a longtime neighbor who is moving away? Wouldn't she love a small album of pictures of the barbecues, holiday parties, and birthday parties you've both attended? Attach a picture of her home to the cover and have the neighbors pose for individual or group pictures.

Make sure your classes coincide with special events and holidays while the enthusiasm is high. Don't forget the smaller occasions, such as Grandparents Day and the First Day of School. All albums don't have to be large. Smaller versions done in a fraction of the time are just as valued.

TEACHING IN STORES

Most scrapbook retail stores offer classes if they have the space. They realize the benefit of having workshops that pull customers into their stores while beefing up sales as well. A scrapper is more likely to buy the newest widget if he knows how to use it from practicing with it during a class. The teacher will spark an interest in a section of the store the customer may have skipped over before due to his lack of knowledge of the product. The coordinated borders, stamps, brads, etc. demonstrated in the class are now "must-haves" for the album pages they wish to replicate.

"Some stores have as many as eight to ten teachers," Stacie Magruder told me. Stacie teaches classes at the Treasure Box in Fort Collins, Colorado. "We normally demonstrate a product and say 'Look what just came in!' You wouldn't believe what they are doing with products," she continued. "Scrapbook stores now offer lines of crafts such as needle and thread, specialty sewing machines, chalk, watercolors . . . you name it."

"You need a professional album to approach a retail store," Staci said. "Fill it full of different styles to show the retailer you can be versatile, using different techniques. Show up with enthusiasm and be outgoing."

If the store already has several teachers, come up with an idea they are not offering in workshop form. How about different hours when the other teachers are not willing to work? Remember, you are selling the store owners a chance to increase their sales by hiring you. Entice them with something and prove to them its benefits to their client base.

You may have to offer to teach at your home if they do not have the space. This could be a great tradeoff for both of you: In exchange for you leaving your cards and advertising in their newsletter, they receive a commission on your classes and may possibly offer you a slight discount on their merchandise for your students. You send them any additional customers that were gained through your efforts, and everybody is happy.

Don't limit your attention to specialty scrapbook retail stores only. Craft stores such as Hobby Lobby and Michaels offer classes on scrapbooking and should be contacted. Now that embroidery and sewing techniques have been added to scrapbooking, it's a good idea to approach fabric stores to offer classes. Be sure to take along album page samples clearly showing how needle and thread are used in today's albums; pique their interest.

WHAT DO I CHARGE?

You will have to talk with the store owner about class fees and splitting the profits for teaching in their outlet. The retailer has all the overhead expense and advertising costs and will want a percentage of the revenue generated through classes.

"At the Treasure Box, we take the cost of the class and then subtract the cost of supplies," Stacie Magruder told me. "For instance, if I charge $20 for class, we first subtract the cost of materials, then divide the profit. I get 75 percent of what's left over and the store receives the other 25 percent."

This formula works if the price of supplies is included in the class. Other ways to charge are to have scrappers pay for the class only, and you supply them with a list of supplies they will need to buy separately. You run the risk of the customers taking the list and buying the supplies at a different store, which undermines your retailer's interest in your workshop. They may also show up with the wrong brand or implement. Make sure they are given the supply list at the time of registration and cautioned that all materials must be on hand for the first class.

The best way to determine your class fee is to see what other teachers are charging in your area for similar classes. If you are collecting store newsletters, you should get a pretty good idea of class fees. Gauge your class charges based on the complexity of the class and the number of hours you will be teaching.

Take a look at your maximum-capacity room for each class as well. If you only have room to seat four people, you will not be generating much income. Most classes try to stay limited to between ten and sixteen attendees. Bear in mind that classes that are too large will cut down on your one-to-one time, leaving the student feeling cheated of your attention and you feeling frazzled as ten hands go up at the same time.

Most classes last roughly two and a half hours, and the best time to offer them seems to be from 6:00 until 8:30 at night.

If teaching from home, obviously you won't have to pay the store a percentage. Your class times may be a bit more flexible as well, as you aren't working around store hours. The square footage you offer for classes from your home will dictate the size of your class.

FINDING CUSTOMERS

If you are teaching at a store, your students will be primarily customers who found out about you through the retail newsletter or other forms of advertisement offered by the owner.

If you are teaching from home and need to find your own client base, there are many avenues you can pursue. We will cover advertising heavily in the next chapter, but for now consider these:

- Ask to leave business cards, flyers, or brochures at scrapbook and hobby stores.

- Many of these stores offer bulletin boards for artists to advertise their classes.

- Ask libraries if you can pin a notice to their community bulletin board.

- Attend as many crops and seminars as possible and offer your cards.

- If your area offers trade shows and expos, you can try to rent a booth or ask the manager of the show if you can offer a demonstration.

- Approach auxiliary stores such as photographers, bridal shops, florists, fabric shops, and children's clothing and toy stores, and ask if you may leave your information.

- Community colleges will let you teach classes if the subject is popular enough.

- What about the places moms frequent, such as gymnasiums, day-cares, sporting events, and schools? Some elementary schools will let you advertise in their newsletters.

- Don't forget church groups and women's retreats.

- Call your Chamber of Commerce and ask that a list of organizations geared toward women be sent to you. These groups are always looking for speakers or seminars.

It would be advisable to offer your students some type of contract, which can include a receipt for their payment. Having everything in writing is always a smart move. Have the contract list exactly what services you are offering for their fee, the hours of the class, and the supplies you are offering, as well as the ones they will need to bring that are not covered in the class cost. You might list additional fees for additional services you offer, should they want to take additional classes at another time. Then, add up the classes they are registering for and enter their check number from their payment or credit card information. List any cancellation policies and refund procedures as well as the deadline to cancel for a class without refund penalties.

Keep a list of your students with their current address and phone number for mailing lists and contact information.

INVENTORY CONTROL

If you do teach from home, you will need to monitor your merchandise and itemize what materials you will need for your classes. That's why it's a smart idea to start out slowly, with one class focusing on one subject. This simplifies your supplies and allows to "get your feet wet" and learn to gauge class needs. As you become comfortable with the number of people attending and what actual supplies are used and what percentage ends up as "scraps on the floor," you can assess what to order and limit your waste.

Always allow for breakage, such as a punch that gets damaged during class time or papers that tear. Have a small "buffer" of materials for the students who will inevitably show up without the requested supply. Charge them at the class time for the "borrowed product," and let them replace it with their forgotten new one or simply pay you and let it go.

As your classes grow in numbers and complexity, order carefully and take into consideration the fact that there will usually be last-minute cancellations. If these non-attendees hurt you financially due to the fact you have already purchased their class kit, then charge them anyway. Have it stipulated in the class agreement form they sign during registration that supply fees are nonrefundable after a certain date. You don't need a lot of leftover inventory unless you feel you can "move" it in future classes.

Keep all inventory stored and organized to reduce damage and confusion. You want to be able to lay your hands on a needed item immediately during class time when the clock is ticking.

Maintain accurate shipping records and record any items you are running low on. Remember, some manufacturers are notoriously slow in shipping, and there are heavy traffic times such as holidays that may delay your orders. Think way ahead and order accordingly. Christmas stock could be depleted by Halloween, so know your vendors and your supplies.

TAKING IT ON THE ROAD

A new concept hitting the market is the scrapbooking party, offered in the same vein as Tupperware or candle or cooking get-togethers. You offer a client a percentage of the party revenue or a "trade-out" in scrapbook supplies based on the number of attendees and total sales. Customers gather at the client's home or business, and you demonstrate your album page layouts and the newest products. If you enjoy being in front of people and love a party environment, consider offering to go into people's homes and show your wares to a select group of scrappers. Your hostess invites her family and friends to see your scrapbooking merchandise and place orders.

You will be expected to demonstrate the uses for the different tools you're introducing to the group. The more ways the implement can be used, the greater its appeal. Don't stick with the manufacturer's suggested use if you can think up some clever alternatives. Its perceived value will increase along with its versatility.

Your display table will be an important part of your presentation. It should be colorful, eye-catching, and well organized. Different levels of display should keep items elevated so that your seated audience can see them. Stack books or small boxes or bowls on the table and drape a small tablecloth or linen napkins over them to display items at varying heights from the table. Add floral arrangements or nostalgic pictures in glittering frames to remind them of the value of albums and legacies. If the party is holiday-based, throw on the confetti, faux snow, and pumpkins. Make it breathe!

Pass things around as often as possible. When items are handled instead of kept at a distance, the "attachment process" kicks in for many shoppers and they "have to have it"!

If time allows, have a worktable where your guests can try out new items for themselves. Seeing something being used for its original purpose can be especially effective.

I did candle party sales a long time ago, and learned something valuable. When the candles were merely lined up in front of an audience, they looked nice and smelled nice, but it was not until they were lit that their importance and beauty came through. Many were designed to have light shine through special cutouts or cleverly layered colors. Others threw unique shadows onto the walls or tabletops. The "oohs" and "ahs" spread throughout the room and the sales increased dramatically.

Be professional in your party sales. Have invoices and business cards printed up with your clever logo and letterhead displayed. If you can afford catalogues or your manufacturer offers them, these are great selling tools. Don't hide the prices—keep them clearly listed, along with the appropriate sales tax. Advertise your promotional plans by inviting those present to have parties of their own and earn scrapbook merchandise. Keep the party fun with games, prizes, and laughter. Refreshments are always a nice added touch.

Look for wholesale manufacturers that will sell you their merchandise in bulk. Then mark it up accordingly and decide if you want to create packages of mixed product to increase sales or sell items singly. For instance, you might put together a kit of paper, punches, and stickers based on a Christmas theme or child's album. The simpler you make it for your customers to create coordinated and attractive pages, the more your sales will thrive.

Limit your party size to no more than ten to twenty people. If it gets too large, the space will feel cramped and your demo area crowded. Large numbers may overwhelm your hostess, and parking becomes a problem.

Evening parties seem to be the most popular when babysitters can be found for little ones or significant others are home from work. Keep the refreshments light and be conscious of drinks that might stain someone's clothes or carpeting.

Use outdated scrapbook merchandise as door prizes and giveaways. Keep it fun and upbeat. Make the display visually appealing in bright, fun colors. It's amazing how much more people will buy if it is displayed or packaged attractively.

Make sure you push your referral program while you're collecting orders. Ask the people attending if they would like to sponsor a party in their home. Perhaps there was a specialty tool they wanted and could not afford at the moment. If so, tell them they could earn it by simply inviting a few friends over to their home some evening. Offer classes to show them how to use the tools they just purchased. You will have shown a short demonstration during the party, but let them know that in-depth classes are available that will teach them exactly how to recreate the pages you've been displaying throughout the party.

A great Web site offering Home Party Plan franchises for work-at-home moms is *www.MyMommyBiz.com*. MyMommyBiz strives to provide moms (and future moms!) with the ideas, resources, and advice they need to make the jump to working from home. On April 1, 2002, MyMommyBiz launched its most ambitious section, Idea Central, which is filled with more than one hundred business ideas and a popluar home party plan business listing. This site offers everything you need to get started as well as financing and setup materials and has a large section on scrapbook endeavors.

SUCCESS TIPS

Stacie Magruder has taught classes for many years and knows what it takes to create a successful class.

"Make sure people are having a good time and not feeling pressured," she says. "Don't offer too many things in one class. It's important for people to leave your class with their pages completed. If too many gadgets and ideas are offered, they can become pressed for time and leave with an uncompleted project."

Keep the atmosphere fun. Your students are coming for more than just ideas on how to create imaginative album pages. "The fellowshipping is important," Stacie emphasizes. "These women are using this time as a retreat from kids and phones and stress. They want to laugh with the lady next to them and exchange stories and ideas. This is their time!"

Have the members of the class introduce themselves quickly and perhaps state why they are taking your class. This not only makes them familiar to the others, but gives you insight into what they are hoping to gain from your class. There may be needs you had not previously thought about, and you can now tailor your class accordingly.

Be upbeat and enthusiastic yourself; your happiness will permeate the class and make the workshop memorable. Laugh with your students and take the time to walk around the room and touch their shoulders as you address them. Make them feel connected and important. Encourage their input and ideas.

Be prepared with everything necessary for the class. A teacher who is hurrying from the room to grab something she forgot or taking time to do the paper folding she should have done before class or finish up the punch-outs will lose the students' interest and waste their time. Know exactly how long your presentation will take to gauge your class time. Include time for interruptions from questions and to work with each student. Try not to consistently run overtime, as a sense of stress will seep into the classroom.

"If there is one thing I wish we could do differently," Stacie Magruder told me, "it would be to offer full-size handouts of the page layouts. The printers for a standard page would have to be 12″×12″, which is a huge printer. I would love to include those printouts in their kits to take home with them, instead of passing a page around for them to look at and return."

Provide as many handouts as possible for the student to take with them, as memories often fail after the workshop is over.

Light refreshments are always welcome and usually provide an energy boost. Some dry types of finger food like cookies, granola bars, etc., might be a good choice. Avoid foods with oils, such as potato chips.

Finally, learn to be patient with the different personalities that will enter your classroom. You will get the "chatters," the "mopers," the "I just can't do this!" types, and the "know-it-alls." If one person is constantly bringing the class down or absorbing time, you may need to talk to her and ask her cooperation or request her removal.

THE COMMISSIONED ALBUM

We've talked about teaching classes, but there are those people out there who have no desire or time to create their own albums and will turn to you for your skill and knowledge. Let's be honest here: You will need to be very good at what you do and offer something special and hopefully different from other commissioned artists out there.

Perhaps you have a quirky brand of humor that makes your trademark or artistic skills immediately recognizable as yours. Having a certain style can land you a lot of business. You may want to specialize in wedding or juvenile albums. Travel albums are big business; most people consider themselves organized if they manage to get their vacation pictures printed. It's a rare person who can take those photos and organize them into an incredible album that fairly screams, "Look at all the fun we had!"

You will need to know color coordination and how to balance elements on a page. There are many good books out there on creating beautiful scrapbook albums. *The Complete Idiot's Guide to Scrapbooking* by Wendy Smedley is very comprehensive and covers everything you could want to know about the art of beautiful and engaging scrapbooks. Internet scrapbook stores also offer the latest in page layout designs. Subscribe to scrapbook magazines such as *Memory Makers, Creating Keepsakes, PaperKuts*, and *Ivy Cottage Creations*.

Your new profession will be creating memorable and enduring works of art. Therefore, your demonstration album must be your best work. You will be dealing with a wide range of personalities and visions when you are dealing with the public. Let your demo album reflect as many themes and styles as you are comfortable with. One client may love rustic country, while another is into something more contemporary and polished.

Include several wedding layouts, including some with humor. Make sure pages dedicated to children and sports are represented, as well as holidays and travel. Again, show your versatility and make it professional; no glue smudges or ripped corners.

The Consultation

"Your customers will have to do some up-front work," says Sharon Colasuonno of Creative Memories. "They cannot simply hand you a box of their photographs and say, 'Make me an album.' You will have to spend some time with them organizing the photos into recognizable groups and by date. How are you supposed to know who the man in the blue baseball cap holding up a twenty-pound bass is? Do they want the pages in chronological order, or by a theme, such as holidays or a certain person only? It would be wise to label the backs of the pictures as you go over them; do not trust your memory on something this important."

You should have a preprinted form of the information you will need when you first sit down with a new customer. Read each item, fill in the information, and check it off. Determine the style they are looking for and, if possible, a budget.

"I am still educating people about albums," Sharon told me. "Many have no idea what 'acid-free' means, let alone 'lignan-free' and 'buffered.' You do more than just reinforce their memories with these albums . . . you are providing protection to their treasured photographs as well."

There are many things that must be found out in this first meeting. Do they want their photos cropped or left as is? Are you to add journaling, or just provide a space for the customer to do her own? How much embellishment are they looking for, and how much are they willing to spend on the different merchandise out there? What about page size? Small album or large, and how many pages were they assuming it will be? How do they want the photos mounted—permanently, or able to be removed for copies, etc.?

Go over your demo pages and point out the different styles, templates, and color ideas. There may be a color they don't like or a combination they've chosen that you know will clash with the content. Don't skimp on the time needed to assess needs and figure clients will be happy with whatever you come up with. This is a highly personal item for them, and their personality needs to shine through.

You will look for customers for your consulting business in the same way you would for teaching classes. We will cover this in great detail in chapter 10, Let's Advertise.

Ka-ching!

What to charge for services in any business is always a tricky subject. I was lucky enough to interview several commissioned scrapbook artists who seemed to agree on an "industry standard" fee scale. They agreed that there are basically four ways to charge for creating an album:

- By the project
- By the photo
- By the hour
- By the single page

In order to charge for the *entire project*, you will have to break down how long you feel the album will take you and then add the cost of materials. Some artists factor in the time they spend at the store picking out the agreed-upon extras, unless they have ample inventory on hand. If specialty items will need to be shipped, include the shipping costs as well. Go over your breakdown with the customer, pointing out the cost of the album itself, the embellishments, and a rough idea of the time required.

By the photo will simply mean counting the number of photographs the client wants incorporated into a scrapbook. You might charge $1 per photo plus whatever embellishments go with it.

By the hour will require you to take a good hard look at what you wish to make per hour for your labor. I found through interviews that $15 an hour was a good average. How many pages can you complete in an hour based on what your customer showed you? Tabulate the number of pages you can create in an hour and divide that number into the total number of pages for the album.

For instance:

2 pages per hour @ $15 an hour = $7.50 per page × 20 pages for the completed album = $150 for labor.

Now add the cost of supplies and shipping (if applicable). This gives you your estimate to present to the customer. Make sure she knows that if she adds pages, the cost will be changed to reflect the new material.

To determine the cost of supplies, you will have to itemize each product selected by the client and add them up. If you are using 12 stickers from a packet of 500, divide 500 into the cost of the stickers to determine what each sticker costs:

Five hundred stickers for $8 would be a little over a penny each. You would multiply your penny and a half by the twelve stickers you will need for that page, or $0.19 for stickers. Add the other elements in the same fashion, including page protectors. You decide if you want to do a small markup on your materials.

To charge *by the page*, you will still need to figure out an hourly rate and the number of pages you can comfortably do in one hour. If you are being asked to create complicated pages, take that into consideration. You do not want to charge the same amount for a simple layout as you would for embossing, folded papers, or pop-ups. Take your time when calculating your fees. More advanced and complicated pages will obviously take more time and more materials. As you do a variety of pages for clients, you will become more experienced at gauging your time and prices.

Toss in the Extras

I cannot emphasize great customer service enough. Do what your competitor is not doing. How about offering a free page for each group of pages ordered over ten? Free delivery and pickup or going to their home for the free consultation would be a plus. Offer extra brads or a specialty item if the order is substantial. Ask if the album is meant to be created as a gift for someone, and throw in wrapping paper or a card. How about a discount for any additional albums offered, or (my favorite), a percentage off for each new client they send your way? I usually figure how much credit I give them based on the price of the new order they send my way. For instance, if the friend they send me orders an $80 album, I would give the referring customer 10 percent, or $8 toward her album cost. It's amazing how many friends they will contact with an impetus like that.

Add a framed picture of little Joey after completing his childhood album. Scan one of the client's favorite photos of her son and surprise her by offering it as a thank-you gift in an inexpensive but tasteful frame. Your name will be shouted to the rafters.

I was asked once to do a charcoal drawing of my friend's wife, who had recently died of cancer. She had been a dear friend to me as well, and I was touched and overwhelmed by the project. I asked for some of the roses from her casket and created a beautiful shadow box containing the flowers and her drawing, along with a poem I created in her memory. I cannot describe the emotion that met that gift. It takes so little to go the extra mile, and yet the impact is enormous!

Get It In Writing

Never undertake the commissioned album without a contract and deposit. Most ask for half down and the balance due upon completion. From this deposit, you can purchase your supplies, unless you have them stocked beforehand. Buy only the products you agreed upon and resist the temptation to purchase extra with a client's funding.

A sample contract is offered in chapter 12, Contracts, Forms, and Checklists. For now, just make sure you have a signed contract in hand before you spend any time in follow-up meetings with the client or purchase anything. Make the contract clear and itemize everything you will be including in the album, the date it is expected, and the number of pages. List any special requests the client has, what materials were left in your charge, and what items are to be returned (if any).

Keep each customer's photos and memorabilia in a separate box and carefully stored while in your care. We are talking about photos and family heirlooms that are irreplaceable. Place them out of the reach of children and pets, possible water damage, and direct sunlight.

THE SCRAPBOOK CONSULTANT

Beneath the umbrella term "consultant" fall many categories. A consultant is a catchall for the other categories we have already discussed. A consultant may be a teacher, a product designer, a commissioned artist, or a seller of product, whether retail or wholesale.

A consultant may be hired to consult with retail scrapbook store owners needing advice on opening a new business. You may be asked to come into an existing store and offer classes on specific new products that come in. You may teach, create, or shop for your client. And the best part is, you can establish a business where you do all of the above.

Creative Memories has built an empire with its direct-sales marketing of its exclusive products and its consultants' expertise. For a set entry fee and purchase of its start-up kit, you are launched with a huge corporation's advertising and support at your back. You receive product discounts that may be enough to keep you happily creating albums of your own while making a profit doing the same for others.

As an independent consultant, you can set up home parties, seminars, trade shows, and retreats. The nation has gone crazy over specialized retreats in the past few years, and they are becoming quite elaborate. Gone are the gym-floor meetings where several people gathered in a reserved room and spread out their inventory while munching on day-old cookies. Now they are whisked off to spas, cruise ships, and mountain cabins. Food and entertainment are included, along with extensive workshops.

The average start-up cost for a consultant is between $300 and $500. This includes basic advertising needs such as business cards, letterhead, and beginning inventory—usually a demo album and extra papers and embell-ishments. Create your own newsletter and circulate it among friends, relatives, and co-workers, or at church get-togethers and hand-selected organization meetings such as ladies' Toastmasters Clubs, or women's golf associations. Contact your local chamber of commerce and ask for a listing of ladies' clubs and organizations or go online for your city's chamber information.

Speaking of cruise ships, these floating entertainment sources are always hiring professionals who offer clientele a trendy way to spend their time. You might approach hotel chains, spas, and daycares with your brochure or sample albums. More on great advertising ideas will be found in chapter 10.

Start out slowly in buying inventory until you get your feet wet with a few sales or clients. If you come across a great clearance sale and you know you can incorporate the merchandise in future sales, then by all means take advantage of it. Buy wholesale whenever possible, which will mean a sales tax license is required. Avoid the urge to stock up on all the cute products screaming at you from the exploding storeroom shelves. Buy your essential supplies such as crop tools, adhesives, pages, etc., and let the extras come in as the need arises.

CHAPTER 9

The BIG Picture!

The scrapbooking industry is one of the fastest-growing craft markets in the world. Each year—in fact, each month—new trends arise demanding more ingenuity to market them and implement them into the customers' expectations. This is all good news to the entrepreneur who not only wants to join the band, but would like a shot at conducting.

This chapter deals with the larger scope of things and offers new avenues open to the scrapbooking business enthusiast.

PLANNING THE SCRAPBOOKERS' EXTRAVAGANZA

There are some adventurous souls out there who have combined their love of scrapbooking with their skills for organization and creative thinking to become scrapbook event planners. Whether designing an event for themselves or approaching scrapbook stores, home-based businesses, and groups, these people are putting on full-scale productions and making a profit from the ticket sales and booth rental charges.

Putting on a larger-than-life production takes many different skills and a lot of patience, tact, and organization. Whether you are organizing a trade show, hosting a large seminar, designing a gala buffet for a scrapbooking convention, or planning a one-of-a-kind workshop symposium, you will have to wear many hats.

Special event planners coordinate. Plain and simple, they coordinate a plethora of details into a polished result. They are paid for their time, creativity, expertise, and attention to detail. The buck stops here when you've been retained to put on a production, which is basically what you are doing.

I've created many elaborate shows in the past years and have loved every minute of it. I adore the brainstorming, designing unique props, and strategizing about the advertising and marketing that will make the event a success. The challenge of doing something different and "jaw-dropping" always appeals to me, and I'm one of those nuts who loves to organize chaos into manageable compartments.

So let's take a peek at some of the areas you will be overseeing if you decide event planning is for you:

- Security: Research, plan, and oversee parking, fire codes, and maximum capacity for your venue

- Technical: Check out lighting, sound, pin lighting, power availability, speaker equipment, A/V setups, special effects, photography, video needs, and staging

- Entertainment: Speakers, workshop teachers, travel and transfers, accommodations and scheduling; breakout rooms, rehearsals, bands or boxed music, and signage

- Décor: Themes, floral arrangements, wall features, ceiling décor, stage plans, stage apron, tablecloths and covers, napkins and trims, invitations, guest tags, etc.

- Venue/Caterer: Site, menu, budget, waiters, beverages, crew meals, tables, chairs, dishware, glassware, cutlery, bars, liquor liability, serving stations, heating and air

- Marketing: Prospect invites, film video, articles, direct mail, promotion, advertising, pledges, sponsors, aim/objective

- Legal: Insurance, permits, licenses, contracts, trademarks, copyright

- Transport: Load in, load out, truck rental, limousine, bus/taxi, air transport

- Staffing: Our team, volunteers, contractors, and committee

- Administration: Timelines, emergency and key contacts, contingency, travel bookings/accommodation, post-event, management fee, stationary extras, phone and fax costs

- Financial: Budget, cash flow, invoicing, statements and accountant

- Miscellaneous: Printing, signage, programs, banners, posters, corporate gifts

Obviously these requirements are for large events. If you are more comfortable planning a neighborhood get-together for ten to twenty people in your home or a hostess's, you will not need to face anywhere close to the number of details just listed.

You may want to brainstorm ideas for holding small, intimate seminars and workshops or crop parties. You select the venue (place where it will be held), advertise the event, decide if you will provide food or drink, and check out the site to make sure you have ample room and outlets, if needed. Tables will be arranged, or chairs if it is a lecture; tools for creating albums can be offered or required for the attendees to bring; and entertainment (if any) can be planned and scheduled. You will check for ample parking and outdoor lighting if your event runs into the evening, and find out all restrictions pertaining to your site, such as nonsmoking laws, seating capacity, fire codes, etc.

Two huge ideas for scrapbooking seminars are retreats and cruises geared specifically to scrapbook enthusiasts.

Jacque from Camp Crop is the perfect example of someone who came up with a great idea and ran with it:

"Camp Crop started in 1997 as a wild idea. My best friend and I thought that a whole weekend away to work on our scrapbooks with no other responsibilities was a great idea. Our husbands laughed at the thought that anyone would pay money to go away for a weekend of scrapbooking. Our first season, we rented a series of vacation homes in Big Bear, California. Each Friday that we had a retreat, we had to drive carloads of supplies up to the mountains. That proved to be too much for my girlfriend, and she bowed out of the business. Believing that I had a still great concept, the next year, I bought a vacation house in the mountains of Wrightwood, closer to my home, and it became the full-time location of Camp Crop. Now we are celebrating our ninth season, and Camp Crop is probably the longest-running scrapbook retreat around. Our home is a full-service bed and breakfast catering to eight scrapbook enthusiasts.

"Because we are committed to providing unparalleled personal attention, Camp Crop has a well-deserved reputation of being a luxurious getaway. Each all-inclusive getaway offers two days and nights of uninterrupted time to work on memory albums. Amenities include gourmet meals and desserts, housekeeping services, popcorn and movies, optional massages, and scrapbook shopping.

"Our best advertising is from word of mouth. Most guests are repeats, and many bring new friends with them each year. We have a Web site at *www.campcrop.com*, which generates a lot of interest."

Retreats need not be held on solid ground alone! The cruise ship industry has weighed anchor on this successful craft craze, and is offering incredible getaways that provide album-creative classes with little umbrellas in the drinks.

Ann Kingrey at *www.getgonecruises.com* enlightened me as to just how much versatility these floating crop shops offer, and how offering fundraisers were a great way to incorporate two loves at once.

"I saw an ad in a local paper about a breast cancer fundraiser a local scrapbook store was doing in Texas (I used to live there). Joan and I are business partners, but also sisters. We lost our mother to breast cancer in January 2002, and we incorporated fundraising into our business. I approached the owner about doing a scrapbook cruise that was also a fundraiser for the Avon Breast Cancer Foundation. Since scrapbookers are mostly women, we thought that would be a good match. She involved other stores in the area, and we were able to sell 100 cabins and raise over $11,000 for Avon.

"We like to sell at least 100 cabins to make the donation to the foundation a good size. However, that is not always possible. We do like to limit the number of scrappers onboard to about 100 people. This makes the group manageable and also easier for class product and goodie-bag donation. A lot of people will bring on friends, spouses, and/or children who don't scrapbook but want to come have a good time."

When asked how she advertises, Ann said, "We have advertised a couple of different ways in the past. We've advertised directly through scrapbook stores, in local papers, and using online advertising like Scrapbook.com and Scrapjazz.com. We have a lot of repeat cruisers and word of mouth. We will also be advertising in scrapbook magazines like *Paper Works*. We also have a cruise set up with PaperKuts that will benefit an autism foundation.

"We've done five- and seven-day cruises before. We have four different cruises planned for next year, each offering a different itinerary. Our cruises range from $446 to $839 depending on the length and time of year of the cruise. We have a five-day scrapbook cruise that is benefiting a SIDS foundation that is $446; our seven-day breast cancer scrapbook cruise in October 2005 is $656, and the PaperKuts cruise in November is seven days and runs from $839."

Offer Something Extra

Everyone appreciates value. Door prizes, giveaways, new product demonstration, guest speakers, and a simple table of treats can make the difference between your event and the dry, regimented one your customers attended last month. Keep the energy level high and add humor. Laughter reduces stress and adds an element of fun. Your enthusiasm will carry over to your guests and make the event memorable.

The way to surprise an audience is to offer something unexpected. For instance, you've provided them with an outstanding event, fulfilling everything you offered in your advertisement; now, there are five minutes remaining in the allotted time and you are thanking them for attending. "Oh! One last thing . . . If you will check beneath your chairs, I believe you will find a small token of my gratitude for attending this event! Once again, thank you for coming, and I look forward to seeing you at my next promotion."

They reach beneath their chairs and find an envelope taped to the underside. Inside is a scrapbooking tool or embellishment, new to the market, and preferably one you introduced to them during the workshop. They now have it to take home and use. Also in the envelope is a schedule of your upcoming events in the form of a refrigerator magnet. Consider the costs of these promotional items when you set your registration fee. You may be able to get a manufacturer to toss in some free merchandise as a way to advertise new products.

You should carefully consider every moment of your event, and try to make it extra-special by taking it up a notch and doing the unexpected and innovative in design, props, entertainment, giveaways, etc. These extra touches have such a great impact that I cannot emphasize it enough. It drop-kicks you up from mundane into extraordinary. Use lots of color and relaxing background music; humor and fun; entertainment if you can; and always, your uninhibited enthusiasm.

Take plenty of pictures and document your events. These can later be submitted to scrapbook magazines spotlighting crops and workshops and showing the reader the latest in innovative events. If it is a larger event, contact the industry magazines and see if they would like to list it or cover it for an article.

You can also use your documentation in ads for trade publications. Crop-A-Lot Retreat was recently advertised in *Memory Makers* magazine. This "Scrapbooker's Camelot" is held in the beautiful Adirondacks of upstate New York. It includes nonstop cropping, prizes, surprises, classes, a diverse tool table, and much more. You can see the company's Web site at *www.cropalot.com*.

Meeting with the Client

As I mentioned in the introduction to this chapter, you can approach scrapbook stores, home-based businesses, and clubs to gather clients for your event. If you have gotten your name out, they may approach *you*.

If you have been hired to put on a large scrapbooking event that requires a special venue such as a rented hall, ballroom, conference area, retreat, or resort, then you will need to be very professional during your meeting with the client. First impressions are critical, and your attire and materials should be polished and professional. Your presentation will speak volumes about what your event will be like: creative and professional versus sloppy and disorganized.

Your Portfolio or Profile

The profile of work is the event planner's major tool in an initial meeting. It contains the record of your achievements, experience, and skill as well as testimonials from previous clients in the scrapbooking world who are singing your praises.

The portfolio should contain pictures of previous events, showing your versatility, the magnitude of the production, and the different styles you offer. Organize your album by themes, clients, or special effects. Take photos from different perspectives, including overhead shots and detailed close-ups. Make the clients feel they are there so they can almost hear the music or excited voices.

The standard display portfolio is 24″×18″ and uses black reversible pages. Since you are in the scrapbooking business, you may embellish your pages, but I would keep it subtle. The emphasis should be on the volume of your work, not the cutesy brads in the corners.

The professional portfolio should contain:

- Career achievements in precise bullet-point form
- Brochures of your professional services
- Photographs of current work
- Testimonials from clients
- Potential client contract and invoices
- Business cards

Always listen carefully to the clients; they usually have firm ideas of what they are looking for. Listen to what is being said between the lines: If the topic of budget comes up often, you may assume that the money allotted is tight and your ability to fulfill the client's needs within a financial perimeter very important. Perhaps a dissatisfaction with a previous planner is alluded to—find out specifically what the problem was and address how you will handle it differently. If you really listen, you will pick up nuances you may play off of and secure the bid.

When it is your turn to speak, keep it concise and to the point, and don't ramble. Let your enthusiasm shine through and pull them into your dream of the event. Personality is a huge seller; don't leave yours at home.

A sample contract checklist and overview sheet will be provided in chapter 12, Contracts, Forms, and Checklists. An excellent book for planning large-scale events is Lena Malouf's *Behind the Scenes at Special Events. How to Develop and Promote Successful Seminars and Workshops* by Howard L. Shenson is another great source.

We will discuss ways to advertise your events in the following chapter, Let's Advertise.

TRADE SHOWS AND EXPOS

A trade show is a large convention open only to businesses in the trade, and requires a business license, resale tax identification, or other proof that you are in a business that would benefit from the show. Some trade setups require you to present your resale tax number and a check showing your business name as proof before allowing you to enter.

At these types of shows, retailers peruse the manufacturer booths to see the latest in merchandise and store displays. These tend to be a little more formal than expos, but can still be stimulating and fun, with door prizes, giveaways, speakers, and entertainment.

Expos are large events laden with booths shouting out their wares to happy scrappers, and are open to the public looking for the newest in merchandise and ideas. Often there are demonstrations, crops, and guest speakers. Activity is high and the expectations huge.

"If event planning requires you to be detail-oriented and a master strategist, so does running expos and trade shows—only more so. The scope of some of these events, in terms of amount of space and capitalization needed, types of contracts necessary, promotional effort required, subcontractors, unions, vendors, and attendees involved, may well exceed anything you've ever done before. Be sure that you have a good idea of what you are about to do before you don the mantle of Expo Impresario." These events must be well coordinated in every detail, and concerns such as guest safety, handicapped accessibility, and parking must be high priorities. A fire marshal will have to sign off on your affair and will examine types of table dressing, room capacity, exits and entrances, and aisle spacing. You will need to check for adequate electrical outlets for the vendors, lighting, air circulation, and monitoring to reduce theft.

Are you offering anything to make the little ones happy, thus making the parents happy? Do you have a play area, strollers, baskets, clowns, face painting, etc.?

Most expos take on an almost carnival-like feel, which opens up the decoration possibilities. Never underestimate the power of visual stimulation when someone enters one of these giant productions. Balloons, ceiling streamers, bold banners, music, and the smell of popcorn or funnel cakes all bring out the wallets and the smiles.

Your advertising should be as aggressive as your client's budget allows. Advertise well in advance, especially during holiday seasons. Prominently announce any special entertainment, door prizes, or guest speakers you will be offering. Perhaps you have booked a popular author in the scrapbook industry and he/she will be signing books during the event. Is there a petting zoo? Are areas provided for workshops or crops? List them all in your advertising. If you're doing radio spots, hit the date and venue address hard. Repeat it often and in a clever way, if possible, so your customers will remember it.

If you want to research other trade shows, there are several Internet sites touting the location and times of upcoming trade shows and events. Go to *www.scraplink.com* for listings of major scrapbook happenings. The HIA (Hobby Industry Association) Trade Show is now called the CHA (Craft and Hobby Association) Trade Show and is usually offered in late January or early February. You can find their information by searching for "scrapbook trade shows" online. The Memory Trends Trade Show is sponsored by *Craftrends Magazine*; their site is found at *www.memorytrends.com*. The Association of Crafts and Creative Industries (ACCI) can be found at *www.accicrafts.org*. Their main show is usually in July. Study these sites to get an idea of trade show and expo requirements, along with contact information, if you are interested in putting on large-scale productions.

SEMINARS

There are scrappers out there wanting more information about their favorite craft. Seminars can be their introduction or emergence into this popular hobby. These can be one-day affairs or weekend retreats. Guest speakers and scrapbook experts abound, as well as ample time for hands-on training. These are structured events, and the timeline must be carefully executed to cut down on wasted time for your teachers, speakers, and guests.

Venues must be canvassed carefully and consideration taken for meals (if offered). Podiums and A/V equipment must be provided for speakers, along with ample room for workshop tables and chairs. Display areas for posters, products, and any other promotional items will be added to your square-footage needs. Leave room for easy movement and those with handicapped needs.

Invite manufacturers to display their products and introduce new lines or upcoming trends and merchandise. Never be afraid to approach these people; you are offering them exposure, and your request generally will be well received. They may charge you for travel expenses, or lay these aside in deference to the size of your audience and their chance to get their product out there. Always get a signed contract and assess their needs ahead of time for microphones, slide shows, etc. Find out how much time they would require and keep them on schedule. Ask how they would like to be introduced and if they will be leaving any promotional material. Decide whether they will be selling their product, or merely introducing it. If sales are a part of their presentation, will they require a credit card setup or petty cash? Will you need bags to carry merchandise home?

Penny McDaniel has invited manufacturers to conduct seminars at her store. "We have had two different manufacturers lead a seminar. The first charged $25 per person, which I passed on to the customer—but no markup for me at that rate! We had a minimum of ten people. The kits she gave out were really good and I was pleased.

"The other did not charge me, but she was not as experienced, and I had to make the kits and samples up, etc."

It's a good idea to find out ahead of time just what your manufacturer is offering in the way of expertise, speaking capabilities, and handouts. Don't get caught off guard once the seminar has begun.

Advertising your seminar will be covered in the next chapter.

HOLIDAY EVENTS

Take advantage of holiday, seasonal, and community events to host a workshop, retreat, or crop. Put together something based on the appropriate theme, rent the space or use your home, send out invites and post notices, and you're on your way.

Christmas, Halloween, and Easter are obvious biggies, but Thanksgiving could be highlighted to play on the nostalgic ancestry note. Scour scrapbook magazines for the latest trends and come up with a few creative ones of your own. Back to School, Father's Day, and Mother's Day can all be expounded upon for sentimental value. What better gift to give a parent than an album commemorating her family? Summer is vacation time, so host a "Vacation Album Extravaganza."

Advertise well in advance for seasonal themes to allow guests to book your workshop among their holiday parties or vacation plans. Detail all the benefits of attending your workshop and play up the joy of a completed album for their recent event while memories and journaling thoughts are fresh. For Christmas, advertise the unique gift-giving quality of an album instead of the standard shirt or canoe paddle. These are presents that will be treasured for generations.

Decide on your venue and how many customers it will seat comfortably, allowing for "roaming" room and a treats table. Create your theme, and design decorations and matching refreshments.

Will you offer tools, or should they bring their own? Are children welcome, or should people please them leave at home? How many ideas will you demonstrate? Will you focus on one style of Christmas page, or offer a few different ideas, varying from antique Victorian to Frosty the Snowman? How about a workshop just for kids to create a small album of the toys they would most like to have for Christmas? Can you imagine how cherished that little book will be down the road when they have graduated from miniature cars to Air Jordan high-tops? The album wish list could be added to each year.

Play festive holiday music in the background and offer some cute giveaway that ties in with your theme. Be creative. If you are doing antique Christmas albums, give each guest a small Victorian fan or skeleton key that could be used on an album page. I love the little "keyhole" keys they sell at flea markets and antique stores. You can sometimes get five for a dollar, and they immediately bring back the feeling of the olden days. Flea markets also sell old postcards from the 1800s and early 1900s, which would add an air of nostalgia and would be completely unexpected and treasured by your attendees.

Use your sense of humor. If your theme is Frosty the Snowman, send each guest home with a small Ziploc bag of giant marshmallows labeled "Snowman Poop."

If the albums will be used as gifts, offer gift tags and scatter creative boxing ideas around the room using—you guessed it, scrapbooking supplies. Don't leave the ribbons and punches on the page; curl them into gift-wrapping bows and sprinkle them across the wrapping paper.

COMPUTER SCRAPBOOKING

If you thought modern technology couldn't touch something as sentimental and hands-on as scrapbooking, think again. Now, without leaving your chair, you can create entire pages complete with photos on your computer, and print them out. The only real manual labor will be the intense effort it takes to slip them into an album. (Yawn!)

David Sutphin is an avid scrapbooker, as well as the owner of Dream Maker Software and the publisher of Cliptures clip art. You can find information about his scrapbooking software at *www.computerscrapbooking.com* and *www.CoolClipArt.com*. David was kind enough to explain just what computer scrapbooking is:

What is Computer Scrapbooking?

"Computer scrapbooking is anything related to using a computer to enhance or create scrapbook pages!

"Most people begin the adventure into computer scrapbooking by using their computer to create design elements that are printed, cut out, and then attached to regular scrapbook pages. Creating text for journaling (captions) and toppers (headlines) is an easy first step. There are a huge variety of computer fonts available that are great for scrapbooking. Using computer clip art is also very popular, and economical too. Two big advantages with both computer fonts and clip art is that their supply is unlimited (you can always print more), and that there is much more flexibility in sizing them to best fit the scrapbook page's designs."

Creating Complete Page Designs

"The next step in computer scrapbooking is creating scrapbook pages on the computer that are printed as an entire page. This is an easy progression from doing print, cut, and paste. The difference is that decorations and text are arranged and formatted on the computer and printed as a single page, except for the photographs and possibly the photo frames. The page is used as is, or the unprinted edges may be trimmed off and the page attached to a complementary backing paper. Regular photographs are still used and are attached to the computer-generated page."

Totally Computer-Generated

"For many people, once they are comfortable with doing complete scrapbook page designs on the computer, this next step is too hard to resist! At this point, not only are the pages being done completely on the computer, but digital photographs are also used so that the complete page, photographs and all, is combined and printed as a single unit. Quality scanners are today very economical, and can be used for scanning old or new photographs, as well as all kinds of memorabilia that can make wonderful additions to scrapbooks. The popularity of digital cameras is growing by leaps and bounds, with many of the newer models offering excellent photo quality. Using scanned or digital photographs also opens a world of possibilities that were impractical or impossible before. Software programs abound that will let you manipulate digital photographs or add special effects in an almost unlimited number of ways!"

And the Future?

"Today, computers greatly enhance and expand the things we can do for scrapbooking, while at the same time making the craft easier and more economical. Digital technology will continue to open up all kinds of new ways for people to create and share scrapbooks. There are lots of fun things just on the horizon, but we'll save that for another time!"

There are many ways you can cash in on this computer-enhanced opportunity for scrapbooking. Obviously, clients could pay you to use your artistic skills and create pages for their albums, either with or without the photographs inserted graphically.

You can create your own ready-to-buy pages and sell them to scrapbook retailers.

How about designing amazing pages and submitting them to scrapbook magazines, or creating a book of your own on how to design and produce your own unique pages?

The Internet awaits you as well: You could sell your pages from your own Web site or entice an existing online retail store. Post your services on their message boards or join chats and tell people about your new venture. In-home scrapbook businesses may be interested in offering your preproduced pages to their clients for a slight markup.

In case you didn't catch it, you can take this new revolutionary procedure into every avenue we've discussed in this book. I realize this technological way of producing a legacy without the adhesive-applied rick-rack, glitter, and buttons is a bit shocking. Let's just say that there is room out there for both what is created by hand and what is created by computer. Many would argue you are creating by hand even when using a computer, since just as many hours are involved to create the page of your dreams.

Some of the software offered for computer scrapbooking includes Paint Shop Pro, Photoshop, Photoshop Elements, Microsoft Picture It!, Corel Draw, and Photo-Paint.

Choose what works best for you and enjoy!

WRITING MAGAZINE ARTICLES

There is money to be made in writing for magazines if you have a talent for the written word and an expansive knowledge of your subject. Just because you can whip out the most impressive album pages known to man doesn't mean you have what it takes to transfer that expertise into writing that will engage a reader.

Magazine articles offer a speedier way to make an income than does writing an entire book. Many women's publications, such as *Ladies' Home Journal, Good Housekeeping*, and others, offer as much as $2,000 an article. The typical craft/hobby magazine will pay a much smaller sum, from $25 on up, or you may be asked to submit your material for free. Look up magazine publishers in the *Writer's Market* (see below) to find a listing of their needs and prices. You will either receive your check upon acceptance of the finished article by the publisher or upon production of the article in the magazine.

A wonderful tool for finding magazine publishers is the *Writer's Market*. This impressive tome contains every publisher in the writing industry in every category, from books to screenplays, greeting cards to magazines. They list the publishing house, its needs, payment policy, the time in which you can expect a reply after your query or complete manuscript is received, titles of recently published works, mailing address, and person to contact.

Always address your query letter or manuscript to the person in charge of the department you're interested in. You will waste your time and theirs by sending it to the head editor unless that person is listed as the one to contact.

A *query letter* is a one-page introduction to what you are offering. In a concise format, you must tell them what your article is about, why you are qualified to write it, why it would appeal to their audience, and roughly how many words it will run. Most magazines have precise guidelines for how long they want their articles to be.

Query letters will either make or break you. If your writing comes across as unprofessional, with many spelling errors, poor sentence structure, or rambling, this tells the editor that your article will likely be just as poorly constructed. You must also, in a brief amount of space, "hook" editors by offering something fresh and innovative. They receive hundreds of queries a week—sometimes thousands. Yours will need to stand out from the crowd.

Study the back and current issues of the magazines you are interested in querying. What has not been offered? What has been offered but would benefit from a new twist? One pet peeve of editors is authors who don't do their research, and send material that is just not appropriate for that publisher. They expect you to have done your homework and respect their time and requirements.

I asked Michele Gerbrandt of *Memory Makers* magazine what they look for in magazine articles. "We have never been 'tapped out' for creative ideas. There are always new ideas. The market (for scrapbooking) is just beginning. You can never have enough talent."

When asked what types of articles seem to be the most popular, she said, "It isn't a matter of what types of articles are most popular, it is a matter of what is coming up on the editorial calendar. Or they (the writer) would look at how our content works and send in something for a specific department."

Michele told me that art ideas included with a query letter are very helpful to give them an overall idea of the article's appeal.

When asked to explain their process of needing articles well in advance for holidays and seasonal issues, Michele informed me that deadlines are six months in advance for all issues, not just seasonal and holiday. "We have two editorial planning retreats a year, and mostly fill in the calendar then for the next six months. Writers interested in submitting query letters should address them to Debbie Mock, Executive Editor, 12365 Huron Street, #500, Denver, CO 80345, or e-mail *editorial@memorymakersmagazine.com*.

Brandi Ginn has been a serious scrapbooker for the past six years and worked professionally for the last four years. She has written numerous articles for *Memory Makers* magazine and is publishing her own idea books with co-author Pam Klassen of *Memory Makers* next year.

I asked Brandi how she approached a magazine for publication.

"My approach was a little different. I had made up a list of article ideas and asked Debbie (Mock of *Memory Makers* magazine) if I could have a meeting with her to go over them. I had been doing freelance artwork for the magazine for about six months prior to our meeting. During our meeting, there were several ideas that Debbie seemed interested in pursuing. The first topic dealt with sewing on pages. She gave me the assignment to go ahead and work on the art for the article. About a week later, I asked her if she'd be willing to let me write the article as well, and she agreed. I was later told that I was the first person the magazine allowed to both create the art and write the article. Having an artist who could also be a writer proved valuable to the magazine, especially in writing art captions. I can look at a page, know how to copy the techniques, and write about them, which gave me an advantage I feel very blessed to have. Things snowballed from there, and I continued to e-mail Debbie with article ideas. After writing a few articles, they started to contact me with their own article ideas that they would want me to research and write. Sometimes I would also provide artwork. I have written all the art captions for two different books, and regularly write captions for each subscription issue and several SIPs (special-interest publications)."

When asked if the publication typically tells her how long an article they're looking for, Brandi said, "Yes, I have always been told how long the article should be. Typically, I'm given a word count for an introduction and told whether or not they would like sidebar information."

I was under the impression that some publications prefer to see artwork separate from the written word, and I asked Brandi if she found that to be true.

"I'm not sure. Whenever I've just written the editors with article ideas, I've only provided the idea. Once I showed Debbie Mock several pieces of artwork that were all 'themed' with the same idea. She ended up publishing all the artwork, but someone else wrote the article. I think that was because the writer had queried her with an idea that happened to go with my artwork. On other occasions where I've been asked to write an article and provide the art, it's never been requested that I show them the artwork before the text or vice versa."

When asked about magazine pay rates and if they pay by the word or the article, Brandi told me: "Over time, my rate for writing art captions has gone up significantly, and I've been thrilled about that. I've never been told if it's by the word; I've always just assumed it's by the article. Once

I researched, wrote, and provided artwork for an article about what adhesives to use when working with 3-D embellishments. For that, I was paid more because more work was involved. For other articles where I've provided one or two pieces of art, I've been paid one rate for the writing and another for the artwork. When I write art captions for the magazine, I'm paid per caption. However, when I wrote all the art captions for the books department, I was paid a flat rate."

When interviewing different scrapbook magazine's editors, I found they were reluctant to comment on the exact fees paid to writers and merely stated that they vary widely. I would recommend querying the different "rags" out there to find out what they are willing to pay for your particular idea.

I finally asked Brandi if she had any suggestions for new writers or artists starting out in the scrapbook magazine submission business.

"I think the best thing for artists to do is to be seen, whether it's layouts posted on the Internet or published in magazines. They should enter as many contests and design team opportunities as possible, take art and design classes, and flat out 'scraplift' other people's work (to practice with). This enables them to see how the creation was made and encourage them to use those techniques in pages of their own. To be honest, I think I got lucky with the writing aspect of this job. I grew up with a mother who is very eloquent with her words and writing abilities. In college, I took advanced writing classes and always did well, but I don't have any formal degree in the subject. I will say this, though. If writers are fortunate enough to be asked to write for a magazine, don't be afraid to ask for help, and *always* ask how you can improve."

SCRAPBOOK MAGAZINE ILLUSTRATION

Magazine editors use mostly staff-created artwork, but they do hire freelance artists with unique styles and fresh, innovative ideas. They will request to see a portfolio of your work. The more versatile you can be, the better. Or maybe you can offer a truly unique style, like the artwork of Mary Engelbreit.

"A scrapbook designer needs to show her work like any graphic designer or illustrator—the more professional the better," Michele Gerbrandt added.

The more proficiencies you have in different areas, the more talents you have to market. For example, Michele noted, "Digital scrapbooking is growing; we just did a special issue on it this summer." So if you have computer skills to combine with your scrapbooking abilities, you can take advantage of this trend.

There are many good books on this market's teaching format, style, and illustrative procedure. The *Illustrator's Market*, companion to the *Writer's Market*, lists all the publishers looking for artwork and their pay scale.

Study the magazines to determine their preferences, but keep a lookout for something different and refreshing you can offer them.

Don't limit yourself to scrapbook magazines. Publications such as *Women's Day*, *Good Housekeeping*, *Martha Stewart Living*, and *Ladies' Home Journal* all run pieces about popular craft trends.

PUBLISHING A BOOK

I will not kid you here—breaking into the publishing world is not easy. You will need something to rival the books already in print. There are more and more books geared to the scrapbooking industry popping up each month. Selling your idea to a publisher will require tempting them with something they know will sell.

Spend some time at your local bookstore or library and scout out the books already on the market concerning your topic. Look at Amazon.com and search for the keyword "scrapbooking." This is a great avenue to use to look at books fresh on the market and find their publishing details: who the publisher is, how many pages the book runs, the date published, reviews, etc.

Buy the *Writer's Market* and check the back section for publishers interested in crafts and hobbies. Then look up each publisher in the book and note what its requirements are. Some will want simply a query letter. You may be asked to submit a query plus two or three sample chapters, or the entire manuscript. The *Writer's Market* will tell you if you will be offered royalties or an advance on your book, and when to expect a response from the editor concerning your submission.

Most royalties for a first-time author run between 4 and 10 percent. The advance can be as little as $100, up to a few thousand dollars. It all depends on the publishing house, how they perceive the value of your book, and whether you have published other books, giving you credibility and bankability.

You can go the self-publishing route, but it is expensive, and you will be in charge of all the advertising, marketing, publishing, and printing costs. The ability to get out and pound some pavement or make waves on the Internet will determine the success of your book. There are many books on the market teaching you how to publish your work. If you plug "self-publishing services" into a search engine, you will unearth a lot of companies that will shepherd you through the process of book production—for a not insubstantial fee. Make sure you do you check them out before you sign a contract.

Also, make sure you have done your research on the books on your specific topic. Many are in full-color detail and were expensively manufactured. Can you top that? What about offering a specialized area of the scrapbooking field, such as journaling, quotes, or poems that album creators could use without copyright infringement? Clever ideas for borders, pop-ups, and holiday specialties would all be good choices. It's hard to run out of great Christmas book ideas. Most publishers are always looking for new holiday books, as so many people collect them.

Check out the *Writer's Market* for advice on writing query letters, how to format a manuscript, and other tips to help you along the publishing path. I have included a sample query letter in chapter 12, Contracts, Forms, and Checklists.

CHAPTER 10

Let's Advertise

*Y*ou can have the best idea or service in the world and not have a single customer if you have not advertised. Before you decide to open a business in any area of the scrapbooking industry, determine your advertising budget and whether you will be able to effectively promote your work. The old saying, "It takes money to make money," is very true. Don't skimp on your marketing if you can help it. We'll cover many avenues for getting your name out there in this chapter, but first, ask yourself this question:

WHAT EXACTLY ARE YOU SELLING?

If we were in a seminar right now and I asked the audience what exactly they would be selling to their customers, the hands would go up and I would receive answers such as: "Albums!" ... "Fancy papers!" ... "Embellishments!" ... "Stickers!" Finally, one hesitant hand way in the back would flutter up, and that person would shyly say, "Memories." *Bingo!*

Someone selling sprinkler parts is not offering his client just some metal heads that squirt water. Without a doubt, the impetus for that customer buying sprinkler heads would include many reasons:

- The pragmatic reason of watering to keep his new sod from dying

- The neighborhood covenants for his new house request a sprinkler system

- He sees how beautiful and lush his neighbors' yards are and he wants a beautiful lawn as well

In my opinion, the final reason is the most important. You are not selling this man irrigation parts, you are selling him his dream of a manicured, perfect lawn that is the envy of all his neighbors.

When bidding on murals and faux painting projects for clients' homes, I realized early on that I was not selling them paint. They were buying elegant walls, a home reflecting their personality, and something that would make their neighbors and friends jealous. Many were buying fantasies for their children in the guise of wall murals and 3-D cutouts.

Look behind the sale: What exactly are they hoping for when they purchase the item?

In the scrapbooking business, you are selling something very personal and dear—a customer's cherished memories and family genealogy. Whether opening a store front or acting as a personal consultant, never forget that.

PLANNING AN ADVERTISING BUDGET

While formulating your business plan, look carefully at what avenues you wish to pursue to effectively promote your business. Would direct mail be the most expedient source to reach your customers, or will you need to spend more money on radio spots or print ads for local magazines?

Set up a budget you can realistically work inside of for the first year. As your business grows, your budget can escalate and incorporate new advertising outlets. Price out the cost of business cards (a must), brochures, flyers, direct mail, etc. The area of scrapbooking you go into will determine your needs.

For instance:

- ◉ Beginning Budget: business cards, flyers, and invoices
- ◉ Intermediary Budget: business cards, invoices, print ads, Yellow Pages
- ◉ Advanced Budget: business cards, invoices, print ads, Yellow Pages, vehicle lettering, direct mail

Call around for estimates and get good value for your money. We'll cover each adverting area below with an example of cost.

PROFESSIONAL CONTACTS

Getting your foot in the door with a professional in good standing in your community is a huge advantage when promoting your new business. Do you know an owner or several owners of scrapbook or craft and hobby stores? Would they be willing to let you post a flyer announcing your new venture? How about a small business card holder with your cards next to the cash register? Could you offer a free demonstration class for their customers, thus promoting your business and increasing their sales?

Contact all stores within a thirty-mile radius or more and tell them you are starting a new business as a teacher or consultant and would like to work out an arrangement with them that would be beneficial to both of you. In exchange for them letting you advertise in their store, you promise to use their products for your classes or send your students to them. You could offer a class gratis in exchange for the exposure.

Whenever you are pitching an idea to an established business, always look at it from *their* point of view. "What's in it for me?" will be uppermost in their minds. What can you offer them that will enhance what they already have, thus making you a desirable "add-on"?

Other contacts will be in-home scrapbookers who hold classes and crops. They would be an excellent source to advertise your new home party line or specialty designs you've come up with.

Approach libraries, colleges, and assisted living facilities to offer classes and promote your products or consulting business. Have plenty of cards to pass around. Assisted living facilities would be a good source for advertising your nostalgic albums to visiting relatives.

Daycares would be another great source, as parents pass through those doors each day and would love an album about little Davey or Sarah. Ask the director about hosting a class for the little ones that will inspire their moms and dads to hire you for a professional book.

If you are pursuing the trade show or expo circuit, you'll want to get in good with the area promoters. Look in the Yellow Pages under entertainment and party planning. Contact these people and let them know you organize special scrapbooking events. Sell them on how big the scrapbooking trend has become, and ask if a section of their next show would benefit from offering a new "draw" for their attendees.

Other professional contacts would be children's clothing stores, gymnastic centers, health spas parents frequent, hair salons, pet stores and veterinary clinics, bridal shops, photographers, framing and matting businesses, and possibly the pediatrics and newborn units of your local hospitals. Anywhere parents, children, and pets are served is a good source for your advertising in the scrapbooking arena.

Kick it up a notch and leave cards at scuba instruction stores, golf shops, camping stores, etc., where people shop for their vacations. Vacation albums are huge, and I guarantee your scrapbooking cards will be the only ones on display in these stores. Think *big*!

YELLOW PAGES ADS

The Yellow Pages ad could be a hit or miss at this juncture of setting up a new business. For one, the scrapbooking industry is still so new that many people don't think to look in the Yellow Pages. Look in your area's phone book and see how many others in your area of scrapbooking are advertising.

A bold-print single line in the Yellow Pages will run you about $40 a month. All you'll receive is the name of your business, address (if desired), and a phone number.

An eighth-of-a-page box ad will cost about $280 and allow you to post your logo, about three to four lines of advertising copy, and your phone number. This allows you to list all that you offer in precise bulletpoint form, along with a small statement such as "Free estimates." You must say a lot in a little space, so choose your words wisely.

Additional perks such as an additional color to make your ad "pop," a larger ad, or more prominent placement will cost you extra.

PLACING DISPLAY ADS IN MAGAZINES

Unless you are offering something that you will want to reach a large audience, the expense of a magazine display advertisement will probably be prohibitive. If, for instance, you are offering your services as a consultant or creating one album at a time for clients, you won't need a magazine ad. Your money and efforts would be better spent in hand-delivered marketing or direct mail.

If you have designed a product or offer your services as an event planner, a magazine ad would be a wonderful venue for you. You will be reaching thousands of scrapbook customers. Make sure you have ducks lined up before you advertise however. Nothing will kill a business like late shipments and unfulfilled promises. If you ad says you ship your product in forty-eight hours, you had better ship your product in forty-eight hours. Have plenty of inventory ready to go.

You will need to offer credit card services if you are dealing with buyers from across the country. Professional shipping materials, invoicing, and tracking methods will also be necessary. You are in the big leagues now.

Advertising in trade journals and magazines can be expensive. Some full-color ads can run you $1,300 on up. The classified section at the back of most magazines is more cost-effective. Check with your chosen magazine for pricing.

Don't limit yourself to scrapbooking magazines. As mentioned earlier, you should consider women's magazines such as *Good Housekeeping* and craft publications such as *Crafts 'n Things* and *Michaels Create! Magazine* (*www.mondotimes.com*).

PLACING PRINT ADS WISELY

Print ads are any ads run in newspapers, magazines, newsletters, catalogues, etc. They are usually boxed and placed strategically within the publication. For instance, you would find a section of the newspaper where your particular talent would be well represented. The entertainment section or local lifestyle section would probably be your best bet. These ads can run into the hundreds of dollars, so assess them carefully.

Newspapers are not high on my list for advertising venues, as they cost a lot and offer a small rate of return. Unless your ad is big enough or really "pops," it may get scanned over by a hurried reader. The rule of thumb for advertisements is that a customer usually has to be exposed to the ad at least three times for it to sink in. This holds true in radio and television, as well as print. That's why it's important to have a budget adequate to do follow-up ads and repeat ads.

"It is true—repetition is the only way," says Penny McDaniel of Legacies. "I used to sell advertising for magazines, and if the client was only going to run an ad once, I would tell them no. You should have a three-time minimum for magazines. Magazines have a long shelf life, and you can get by with a minimal number of ads. Newspapers, however, are a different thing; you need to get to a point of brand recognition which means running the same ad over and over and over. You will get tired of it long before the public will."

Local or area magazines are a good between, as they are delivered within a certain demographical area. Many of these publications are open to bartering, and may be willing to run your ad in exchange for a family album.

Contact retailers who sell scrapbook, craft, and hobby supplies, and see about advertising in their newsletter. This should be pretty cost-effective and go straight to your customer target market.

Check with catalogue companies that mail out seasonal publications replete with merchandise for the hungry holiday crafts person. Do you have product you could sell through their mailings? For example, Lillian Vernon is a huge seller and offers a variety of products.

DIRECT MAIL

In order to utilize advertising through direct mail distribution, you will first need to compile a database of customers. If you are just starting out, you will need to be creative in finding names for your mailers.

Start with friends, family, church members, daycare acquaintances, health club buddies, your hairstylist, etc. Compile a list of names, addresses, and phone numbers. You can visit local crops and scrapbook Web sites selling supplies to see if you can utilize the chat rooms or message boards to acquire new names. Whether Web sites will welcome you will depend on what service you are advertising. If you are competing in their arena, odds are they will tell you to take your albums and hit the road.

Once you have a list of names compiled, design a postcard or flyer to be mailed out. Most direct mail companies in your Yellow Pages will be happy to tell you their mailing restrictions, size of the mailer, postal regulations, etc. Your design should be simple, with bold letters announcing the topic to make it stand out from other mailers. The competition to get noticed is high here. The direct mail companies can consult with you on how to achieve impact, and many offer design services. Look under Mailing Services in your Yellow Pages for those that offer full service design and delivering. Ask your local graphic designer for a few clues, or study the mailers that come in your mail. Which ones jump at you and which are lost in the bulk? Visuals always add punch, and most people will notice a picture before they read the print.

If you want to blanket a certain geographical area, you can look up mailing list companies in the Yellow Pages, and they will sell you mailing lists for a specified demographic area. You can choose the income level of homeowner you are looking for, specific subdivision, or any number of combinations. A typical fee for 5,000 mailing labels is around $185. These lists are updated periodically to insure you have an accurate mailing.

It will be up to you to update your own lists. As customers move or are no longer interested in receiving mail, make the appropriate changes. Add new clients as they appear, and always ask if they have a friend or relative who might be interested in receiving scrapbooking news.

"We sign customers up when they check out at the register," Penny McDaniel told me when I asked her about her mailing list ideas. "Their names go directly in my database. We also have a drawing, etc. and get names and numbers that way. I do a bi-monthly newsletter (about six to eight pages) with our calendar of events for the next two months. It's another thing I think is interesting in this industry: Store owners started the whole newsletter thing, and now it is not a value-added service for the customer—it is expected! I don't know if that is a good thing or a bad thing."

ORGANIZATIONS

Your local chamber of commerce has listings of every organization that meets on a regular basis in your town. This list is free for the asking and is updated regularly. Here you will find women's groups, men's groups, senior citizens, equestrians, butchers, bakers, and candlestick makers.

Call the contact person listed with the group you would like to target and tell her you would be interested in offering a free class or seminar to the group to demonstrate the incredible world of scrapbooking. These groups are always looking for fun things to do to entice their members to come out regularly to meetings. Once you're before the group, you can hand out cards and flyers, or even sell products if the committee agrees to that.

Don't limit yourself to women's groups. Contact agencies that work with teens and children. Crafts are often offered in rehabilitation settings or to help troubled adolescents. Try your local Boy and Girl Scout dens and offer to teach a class.

Men's groups would be interested in an album showing their sporting achievements, hunting expeditions, company awards, etc. If Valentine's is near, offer to help them make something sentimental and special for their sweethearts.

Professional organizations could be a gold mine of customers. Your local Home Builders Association would welcome an album of their custom homes to show prospective clients. Hair salon and beauty clinics all show albums, as do pet organizations and such specialty areas as equestrian shows.

SPECIAL EVENTS

The holidays are full of craft and hobby shows. Get permission to hand out cards or flyers at these functions. You may be charged a small fee or required to have a permit (usually a $10 cost) to offer any type of advertisement at these types of promotions. Concerts, sporting events, carnivals, and any large-scale event being offered in your area are bonanzas for being able to reach a vast number of people.

You may want to set up a simple booth displaying your albums or merchandise with your business cards and brochures prominently displayed. Check with the event organizer and ask about fees and visibility. You will be wasting your money if they stick you off in some corner.

THE INTERNET

The Internet literally places your wares and services before the world. The number of people you can reach via a Web site is mindboggling. Chances are, your Web site, outfitted with the right keywords and metatags, will show up every time a happy scrapper types "scrapbooking" into her favorite search engine.

You can decide whether to have your own Web site touting your services as a consultant, commissioned album artist, or event planner, or open a store offering the latest in merchandise and layouts. You might want to show off your newly patented creations and open your doors to orders.

If posting your offerings on site message boards is more your speed, those opportunities abound. Most scrapbook retail sites offer message boards and chats. Take advantage of them. Many of these stores also offer e-mail setups and group links. Scrapping4others at *http://groups.yahoo.com* is a great site for hooking up with others and learning marketing strategies and many other informative tips of the trade.

REFERRALS

Let's face it—word of mouth is always the best advertising. You have satisfied customers out there bragging about you and "selling" you to their friends. No job is too insignificant not to do your best. Often it is those small jobs that sing your praises the loudest: "She took so much time on this when it was such a small commission. That says a lot about someone, when most people only want the big jobs."

Offer a referral program at every opportunity. If you are commissioned to create an album for a client, offer her 10 percent off her next purchase or some free pages for each customer she sends you. It only takes a moment of her time to tell someone about you, and she reaps the rewards.

Obviously, the scrapbook party line is all about generating referrals and picking up new customers at the party. Send them forth with your handcrafted banner flying to proclaim your worth to the world . . . or at least the neighborhood block.

If you've planned an especially successful event, ask the vendors to spread your name or use you for upcoming shows.

"You're only as good as your last job" is a saying to think about. Make sure the word circulating about you is a good one . . . or on second thought, a *great* one!

PROMOTIONAL MATERIALS

Promotional materials are anything you leave or pass out to advertise your business. The more cleverly constructed they are, the more they are used, kept, and remembered.

Creative packages of your specialty designer paper and stickers can be left with retail stores to show customers and take orders. Your sample album, spread out on a table at a bridal salon with brochures next to it, makes a great promotional item.

Flyers pinned to the library bulletin board or delivered to craft shows and scrapbooking workshops are a great marketing tool. Refrigerator magnets listing your skills, workshop dates, and phone number are always kept and in front of your customer, reminding her about you on a daily basis.

Do the unexpected. Copying someone else's design or concept will only make you a "cookie-cutter" duplicate. Blow their minds, and you'll capture their attention and their business. If you are trying to land a corporation's business, don't just show up with a generic flyer or brochure and say, "Would you please make sure Mrs. Carlson gets this?"

Instead, bring in a clear inflated Mylar balloon with your flyer rolled up inside. Fill it with tiny punch-outs or scrapbook confetti and tape a pin to the outside. Believe me, when the person in charge pops that balloon to get your missive, she *will* remember you and be impressed with your ingenuity.

Make your business cards clever and memorable. People tend to hold on to a great card whether they think they'll need it or not.

TRADE SHOWS AND EXPOS AS A MEANS OF ADVERTISING

We have covered trade shows and expos in some detail in chapter 9, The BIG Picture!, as one of the many career fields under the scrapbooking umbrella. Here we address it as a means of advertising your business.

Obtaining a booth at one of these conventions is a surefire way to get your name, product, or service out there. Most booths will run anywhere from $150 on up, with about $380 to $400 being a common fee. For that amount, you will receive a basic table and chair, an electrical outlet, and possibly a partition. Anything extra, such as easels, additional tables and chairs, etc., will cost you. You are expected to bring your own banners, signs, and sometimes table draping if not included in the price of the booth.

Most trade shows are very explicit about what constitutes your "area." You are not allowed to walk but a few feet from your booth to hand out flyers to the passing masses, and any extra attractions, such as putting greens or costumed characters, must stay within the prescribed perimeters. You must be in attendance at your booth at all times, and if you have items like scissors, you are responsible for the safety of your booth guests.

Any items that might damage the conference setting floor will have to pass scrutiny. Water features, adhesives, sharp corners on your furnishings or props, etc., are open for a judgment call. Since others at these shows are all required to pay for their booths, it is illegal for you to just show up and hand out promotional materials to attendees. You can ask whether the show will allow you to do that for a fee, but don't try to do it otherwise. Slipping flyers under vehicle windshields at these expos is also iffy, so you should check with the show coordinator.

NETWORKING

Attending organization meetings and fundraisers is a great way to drum up business. The time-honored "passing of the cards" is always prevalent at these get-togethers. "You scratch my back and I'll scratch yours" is still in good standing.

Take plenty of cards and listen attentively to what others there are offering. It's common courtesy and can often lead to opportunities you had not thought of.

Find out where crafters and hobbyists meet; check your list from the Chamber of Commerce and ask around at the applicable stores.

THE STATIONERY END OF THINGS

Your letterhead stationery, business cards, invoices, flyers, and brochures will all shout bundles of information about who you are and what you are. What you want to be is professional.

Spend a few extra dollars to have your letterhead printed at the top of your invoices instead of just penned in one at a time. Have your contracts professionally printed unless you have a good software program with graphic and font capabilities. Today's computer packages can produce some pretty amazing results for as little as $19.99.

Your business card should be well thought out and professionally done. Print shops such as Kinko's offer a graphic artist who will help you with the layout of your cards, flyers, brochures, etc. and print them out. A box of 500 cards can run as little as $150 for a two-color layout. Embossing, fancier card stock, or additional colors will elevate the price.

Kinko's and other copiers also offer a wonderful array of specialty border papers that you may purchase, adding to them your advertising copy. For $4.95, you can buy 25 sheets; some are laid out two sections to a sheet, giving you 50. For under $5, you will have 25 to 50 flyers with beautiful borders and backgrounds to hand out, instead of spending hundreds on a full-color press setup.

With your letterhead stationery, use matching envelopes. If you're using white paper, don't slip it into a beige envelope. Professionally printed thank-you cards are also nice to add to your office supplies.

CHAPTER 11

If You Have the Passion, You Have the Potential!

*I*f there's one thing I'm sure of, it's that passion fuels any vehicle headed for success. You can try to get by on fumes by approaching your goals with a half-hearted attitude or get a push when your pessimism stalls you in the middle of the road, but if you're serious about taking this dream of yours all the way, there's only one way to do it—with the correct motivation.

MOTIVATION

I've been self-employed for over twenty-six years now. In that time, I've learned that when you work for yourself, you have to be able to motivate yourself. Sometimes that motivation comes in the form of making just one more phone call to a manufacturer to secure the best price for your products. It may mean teaching a class when you don't feel well or when there is an especially tiresome student who attends each week. Perhaps you lack the motivation to get out there and advertise or market your wares.

Being alone at home can be a little daunting if you've been used to having a boss tell you what to do, when, and how fast. Now you're in charge of scheduling your time and setting the bar. How much you accomplish will be determined solely by your efforts.

Many new entrepreneurs find it difficult to become self-starters and discipline their activities. The temptation to vacuum first, make a quick call to your sister, or run an errand all tug at your elbow as you try to start your day. Do yourself a favor and make a list the night before of the things you need to accomplish the following day. Put down a rough time slot to encourage you to stay on task. For instance:

8–9:30 A.M.	Type mailing labels for direct mail
9:30–12 noon	Distribute flyers to Michaels, Hobby Lobby, and Betsy's Album Den
12–1 P.M.	Lunch

1–2 P.M.	Call manufacturers and ask about shipping costs
2–3 P.M.	Organize inventory
3–5:30 P.M.	Crop workshop

It helps to have a support group encouraging your efforts. This may be your family or a good friend. These people are there to say, "Keep going, you're doing great!" It means so much to know you are not alone as you start a new endeavor. Tell them that their support is appreciated, and be there for them when they need a boost. Set up your office or surroundings with motivational elements such as uplifting music, your favorite beverage, inspiring messages posted around your computer, etc. I have two quotes pasted to my computer that I read every day: Thoreau's "If one advances confidently in the direction of his dreams and endeavors to live the life which he has imagined, he will meet with a success unexpected in common hours," and Victor Hugo's "Nothing is more powerful than an idea whose time has come."

I am a strong believer in the power of positive projection. Take thirty minutes each morning, find a quiet place, and "get still." Take three very deep breaths, let them out slowly, and release your mind to wander the universe. In that short amount of time, ideas and inspiration will come to you, along with a wonderful peace of mind. I look at it as fuel for the soul. See yourself as successful and your business thriving. Envision it all—your office, workshop, or retail outlet. See the orders coming in and the happy customers singing your praises. What will you be wearing? What vehicle are you driving? How are you arranging your store? What vacation will you take to celebrate your success?

It's important to imagine it all happening *now*—not down the road. See the abundance flowing into your life now and joyously accept it. Go through your days with a bucket to catch all the miracles and wonderful things coming into your life. I prefer to drive a flatbed truck to catch all mine, but a bucket will do to start with!

On the days that things seem slow and you feel yourself getting discouraged, take action! Make some phone calls to organizations you have not tapped, hand out flyers, design a new brochure that adds more sparkle. Visit scrapbook stores and notice the new merchandise or chat with some of the customers or the owner. Go on the Internet and enter some chat rooms to talk with scrappers there. These types of activities keep you busy and generate positive energy, which in turn makes things happen.

Call on your support team if you're blue, and go to lunch. Nothing gets you back on your feet like a good old-fashioned pep talk.

Just remember, all businesses go through slumps. Don't take it personally. Some times of the year are just busier than others, and there seems to be a rhythm to the days. Go with the flow and try not to take it seriously. You'll find if you talk to other businesses in your field that they are probably experiencing the same slowdown. It will pick back up again, and you'll be wishing you had a chance to breathe.

OFFERING MORE THAN YOUR COMPETITOR

Two summers ago, my teenage son passed out flyers in our subdivision advertising his new service as pet sitter, lawn mower, snow shoveler, and house sitter. He got quite a good response, and the repeat business has carried him through two summers now. One of the neighborhood boys noticed my son's success and began passing out his own flyers. When I was apprised of the situation through frowns and sighs, I told him that he should expect competition in all areas of life, and the secret was to offer something better than the next guy. Since he was already doing a bang-up job with his customers, I recommended an added touch. He made homemade chocolate-chip cookies and placed them on a paper plate with a note that read "Welcome Home." When his customers returned from vacation, they found the wonderful treat waiting for them. Guess who they call every time they need anything?

When clients ask him to pull weeds, my son will usually do something extra, such as carry trash cans to the end of the driveway, hose down walkways, or prune a few bushes. I am pleased that he's learned at such an early age the value of service and going the extra mile. He often receives bonuses and gifts for his efforts. People really do appreciate being cared about, and the fact that they are not just a paycheck.

GOAL-SETTING

I'm a big advocate of making lists for goal-setting. You will need to make short- and long-term goals. The great feeling you receive from checking things off your list will make you eager to continue on.

Take a sheet of paper and entitle it "Short-Term Goals." List the goals you would like to accomplish in the next month. Take the last day of the month and then work backwards, listing what bite-size things you need to accomplish each day in order to achieve that goal. Keep them manageable so that you don't become discouraged.

Your goal may be to bring in at least ten new customers. Based on whether you own a store, have a home-based business, run an Internet site, or work as a consultant, you will determine what marketing strategies you will need to employ. Now, beginning with the last day of the month, go backwards week by week or day by day. The last week will probably be meeting with the new customers. Week three will be follow-up phone calls from the business you just generated. Week two is distributing flyers, running radio spots, kicking in a new promotion, or circulating newsletters. You may run a special on your Web site or contact professionals who can send business your way. Week one is planning your advertising strategy and designing the ads, etc.

By working backwards, you're assured of meeting your target deadline. Authors use this technique, as well as seminar planners and event coordinators.

Use this same strategy to plan out long-distance goals, breaking them into manageable months. Having a game plan will assure success more than flying by the seat of your pants.

I HAVE TOO MANY ORDERS . . . NOW WHAT?

There may come a day when you will need to hire additional help. Carefully factor in employee salaries, benefits, insurance, etc. You will also be taking on additional paperwork for Uncle Sam. Look in chapter 3 for a breakdown on legal requirements when taking on a staff.

If your inventory is outgrowing your garage, basement, or back room of your store, it may be time to look for a new location. This is a critical move and should be done after much deliberation. Don't jump into more square footage than you need. Perhaps you don't need a new location as much as you need extra storage space. Is it more cost-effective to rent a storage unit for excess inventory, or even remodel your current setup? Perhaps a member of your family or a friend has a large amount of basement space she would be willing to rent to you. Can you use a spare room in your house, or organize your storage bins to be more effective and space-saving?

Another option would be to outsource your product needs to a manufacturer in this country or overseas to make some of the parts, or all, in quantity. The Asian market is a huge source for inexpensive manufacture of small to elaborate pieces. The popularity of having another factory create wares can be seen in the growth of importers in this country who are playing middleman to make a profit on overseas orders.

Compare everything before you put a "For Sale" sign on your store, and shop around for a retail location if you've been working from home. Make sure you can afford the overhead and a delay in business while you set up your new shop.

IT'S NEVER JUST A BUSINESS!

There are few businesses out there that touch home as much as the sentimental art of scrapbooking. This is *not* just a business . . . It's a means of ensuring the photographs and memorabilia of your customers' loved ones and life experiences are kept together and protected. Never forget that. The ringing of the cash register should be secondary to the customer service you offer and the repeat business generated because of it.

Keep your enthusiasm and passion for your trade alive by offering stimulating workshops, marketing, and in-store gimmicks. The fresh atmosphere and fun environment will keep you feeling engaged, as well as your clientele.

I wish you all the best with this exciting new venture of yours. Be proud of yourself for being a risk-taker and pursuing your dreams instead of sitting on them.

One last thought: Keep an album of this journey, documenting all the steps you took to arrive at your successful opening of your new business. Then add the pages as your days grow in prosperity, and add a well-deserved pat on the back!

All the best!

CHAPTER 12

Contracts, Forms, and Checklists

DIFFERENT CONTRACTS FOR DIFFERENT SET-UPS

Commissioned Album Contract: Sample

Scrapbooks by Michele
5897 Miramont Drive
San Diego, California 92045
(800)555-7890
scrapbooksbymichele@aol.com

Client Agreement

Client _____ Date _____

Address _____ Phone _____

Description of project _____

Date of concept _____ Date of completion _____

Estimate _____ Half down _____

Balance due _____ Delivery or pickup? _____

Client provided the following items: _____

_____

Special requests: _____

I agree to the following conditions:

1. I will provide photographs, memorabilia, and other items to Scrapbooks by Michele for inclusion in the commissioned album. These photographs will be mounted using only adhesives, papers, etc. that will not damage my items. If I should provide

poor-quality photos or clippings causing "acidic bleed," etc., Michele will not be held responsible. I will inform her of any photos that are irreplaceable and have no negatives.

2. I understand the items I present to Scrapbooks by Michele will be stored in a safe environment and every precaution taken to insure their safety. I will not hold her company responsible for acts of God such as floods, hurricanes, tornadoes, etc. resulting in damage to my property.

3. I will inform Scrapbooks by Michele of any photos or memorabilia that I do not want permanently affixed to the album page. These items will be mounted using photo-safe corners for easy removal. These will be labeled as such or included in a separate envelope or inventory sheet.

4. Michele has my permission to crop any of the items I've presented to her to facilitate placement and balance. Those I do not wish altered have been so marked and included on the inventory sheet.

5. A half-down deposit will be required up front to purchase the album(s), supplies, etc.

   As materials will be purchased with this money, it is nonrefundable. The balance will be due upon completion and satisfactory acceptance of the album and its contents.

6. All shipping charges, if applicable, are included in the bid. Scrapbooks by Michele will take full responsibility for choosing a reputable carrier and purchasing adequate insurance with proof of delivery required. In the event of a mistake by the carrier, the burden of replacement and damages will fall upon the agent.

7. I will request any unused materials to be returned to me and check them off the inventory sheet. Scrapbooks by Michele will happily deduct from the balance due any cost of materials not used in the project or offer me said items for my use.

8. I authorize Scrapbooks by Michele to use scanned images of my pages for future advertising. _____ I do not authorize Scrapbooks by Michele to use scanned images of my pages for future advertising. _____ (Please check one.)

I have read and agree to all conditions listed above. My satisfaction is guaranteed based on the information and supplies I've provided. Any changes added after the completed album is delivered are subject to additional charges if these fall outside the range of the original concept.

Client _____ Date _____

Scrapbooks by Michele _____ Date _____

Michele Stauffer

Contract Requirements for Events Checklist: Sample

1. The name of the event

2. The names of the parties entering into the agreement

3. A billing clause

4. A cancellation clause

5. The fee

6. Payment terms

7. The venue information

8. The date of event

9. Contracts and clauses for other vendors (caterers, entertainers, etc.)

10. Travel arrangements

11. Accommodations

12. Estimated attendance

13. Parking requirements

14. Special A/V requirements, electrical outlets, special effects, etc.

15. Time and duration of event (includes take-down and cleanup)

If you are multitasking and doing more than one area of scrapbooking for profit, i.e., you are a retail store owner and a consultant, add categories of earnings, i.e., Consulting, Teaching, Sales, etc., to this ledger.

BOOKKEEPING FORMS

Daily Accounting Ledger

Day _____   Month _____

Income					
Total					
Expenses					
Rent					
Utility					
Phone					
Debt Payments					
Advertising					
Salary/Wages					
Maintenance					
Supplies/Office					
Inventory					
Vehicle Expense					
Insurance					
Shipping					
Payroll Taxes					
Employer Taxes					
Benefits					
Legal Fees					
Other					
Total					
Profit					
Cumulative Total					

Weekly Accounting Ledger

Month of: _____

	Week 1	Week 2	Week 3	Week 4	Week 5
Income					
Total					
Expenses					
Rent					
Utility					
Phone					
Debt Payments					
Advertising					
Salary/Wages					
Maintenance					
Supplies/Office					
Inventory					
Vehicle Expense					
Insurance					
Shipping					
Payroll Taxes					
Employer Taxes					
Benefits					
Legal Fees					
Other					
Total					
Profit					
Cumulative Total					

Your monthly accounting ledger is the same setup you will use for your profit and loss statement.

Monthly Accounting Ledger or Profit and Loss Statement

Year Of:_____

	Jan	Feb	Mar	Apr	May	June	July	Aug	Sept	Oct	Nov	Dec.
Income												
Total												
Expenses												
Rent												
Utilities												
Phone												
Debt Payments												
Advertising												
Salary/Wages												
Maintenance												
Supplies/Office												
Inventory												
Vehicle Expense												
Insurance												
Shipping												
Payroll Taxes												
Employer Taxes												
Benefits												
Legal Fees												
Other												
Total												
Profit												
Cumulative Total:												

THE BUSINESS PLAN

A Sample Table of Contents

Section One: The Business

    A. Description of Business

    B. Product/Service

    C. Marketing Information

    D. Location of Business

    E. Competition

    F. Management

    G. Personnel

    H. Application and Expected Effect of Loan

    I. Summary

Section Two: Financial Data

    A. Sources and Applications of Funding

    B. Capital Equipment List

    C. Balance Sheet

    D. Break-Even Analysis

    E. Income Projections:

        1. Three-Year Summary

        2. Detail by Month, First Year

        3. Detail by Quarter, Second and Third Years

        4. Notes of Explanation

F. Cash Flow Projections

1. Detail by Month, First Year

2. Detail by Quarter, Second and Third Years

3. Notes of Explanation

PERSONAL CHECKLIST

- ❏ Decide which area of scrapbooking you want to go into.

- ❏ Take a look at your fears and decide how to attack them.

- ❏ If you are opening a home-based business, how will your family deal with it?

- ❏ How are your finances?

- ❏ Are you a good candidate for a loan?

- ❏ Can you handle stress?

- ❏ Would you make a good boss? Can you delegate? Could you fire an employee?

- ❏ Can you handle a retail setup and the decisions it requires?

- ❏ Do you need to attend business classes or seminars before opening your business?

- ❏ How is your wardrobe?

- ❏ Are you organized? Are you a self-starter?

- ❏ Are you good at bookkeeping?

BUSINESS CHECKLIST

To-Do Checklist to Get Started

- ❏ Check zoning laws
- ❏ Register your name with your state's Department of Revenue
- ❏ Obtain sales tax license and other permits
- ❏ Obtain your quarterly income tax forms
- ❏ Buy insurances for business: liability, personal property, etc.
- ❏ Have business cards printed up
- ❏ Set up bank account
- ❏ Buy or create invoices in two- or three-part carbon sets
- ❏ Take your vehicle to be lettered
- ❏ Put together your sample album and portfolio
- ❏ Purchase inventory
- ❏ Purchase storage bins and display racks for inventory
- ❏ Set up your answering machine or voice messaging
- ❏ Buy a cell phone if you don't already have one
- ❏ Create your flyers or direct mail layouts
- ❏ Order your Yellow Pages ad
- ❏ Set up your office with computer, fax, copier, and printer
- ❏ Set up file cabinet
- ❏ Subscribe to scrapbook magazines
- ❏ Check out your wardrobe for professional clothing additions

Retail Owner's Checklist

- ❑ Find a reputable real estate agent or locate a store front yourself
- ❑ Consider buying an existing business or franchise
- ❑ If in a mall or plaza setting, find out the covenants and restrictions
- ❑ Sign lease and put down deposit
- ❑ Remodel if needed, and decorate
- ❑ Order any fixtures, display cases, workshop tables, etc.
- ❑ Sign up for your utilities and phone hookup
- ❑ Set up your point-of-sale system
- ❑ Contact your suppliers
- ❑ Hire an accountant and set up your accounting and bookkeeping
- ❑ Order signage
- ❑ Order inventory
- ❑ Price and stock inventory
- ❑ Interview carrier services
- ❑ Interview employees
- ❑ Hire employees
- ❑ Stock break room and bathroom supplies; cleaning needs

SAMPLE QUERY LETTER FOR BOOK PUBLISHING

Sharon Davies
3455 Vista Way
Mount Seanna, WA 89765
(800) 555-6544

Patricia Cornley
Welshford Press
1345 Avenue of the Americas
New York, NY 10017

Dear Ms. Cornley:

My name is Sharon Davies, and I am writing you with a proposal for a 40,000-word book entitled *Scrapbooking for the Generations.*

With the current explosion of popularity in the scrapbooking industry, the need for innovative books on this topic has never been greater. Research into family genealogy continues to grow and fuel the need to create meaningful, time-sensitive albums.

In *Scrapbooking for the Generations,* I will disclose the most effective tools for finding your ancestors through today's modern technology. The archives in the Salt Lake City office of The Church of Jesus Christ of Latter Day Saints, along with Internet facilities, will allow the reader to launch an effective program for discovering his heritage.

Part Two of the book will offer never-before-seen layouts and themes to catalogue this information and document it in visually appealing pages. Thus, in one purchase, the reader will acquire the skills to fill in the branches of his family tree *and* preserve it for generations to come.

I have been researching genealogy and scrapbooking techniques for over ten years now and have published articles in archive trade journals and craft magazines; clippings of these are included with this query letter.

Thank you for your time in considering this book proposal. If timing is everything, then I believe the timing for this particular subject and treatment has never been better.

Warm regards,
Sharon Davies

References

SCRAPBOOKING STORES

Legacies: Photographs and Memories
1425 No. Denver Ave.
Loveland, CO 80538

Your Crop Shop
12850 West 64th Ave., Unit K
Arvada, CO 80004
(303) 463-8591
YourCropShop@msn.com

The Paper Attic
9433 So. 700 E.
Sandy, UT 84117
(801) 523-1990

Addicted to Scrapbooking and Addicted to Rubber Stamps (Internet store)
David.Kovanen@Innovator.com

The world's largest online retailer of rubber stamps and scrapbooking supplies. Over 250,000 items in stock: Order Today-Ship Tomorrow. Satisfaction Guaranteed or your money back. *www.AddictedtoRubberStamps.com* and *www.AddictedtoScrapbooking.com*.

CoolClipArt.com (Internet store)
www.coolclipart.com

Computer Scrapbooking (Internet Store)
www.computerscrapbooking.com

SCRAPBOOKING SPECIAL EVENTS

Get Gone Cruises
www.getgonecruises.com
Ann Kingrey, ACC
ann@getgonecruises.com
(866) 443-8466

Camp Crop
www.campcrop.com
Jacque@campcrop.com
CHA Show: Craft and Hobby Association Trade Show
www.CHA.com

Memory Trends Trade Show
Sponsored by *Craftrends Magazine*
www.memorytrends.com

ACCI Crafts Trade Show
www.accicrafts.org

BUSINESS HELP WEB SITES

LegalZoom.com
Trademark, Copyright, and Business professionals
www.legalzoom.com

Invention Home
www.inventionhome.com
1-866-THINK-12
info@inventionhome.com
Russell Williams
Invention Home is striving to build the largest invention-marketing network in the United States with their patented (pending) invention marketing method. They help independent inventors to develop and market their ideas/inventions with patent and invention marketing-related services. Invention Home is a family of inventors who succeeded in the invention industry by developing their own product into a multi-million-dollar product line consisting of over sixty product SKUs.

Neustel Law Offices
Patent Attorneys
www.patentapplications.com

BFI Business Filings Incorporated
The Internet Leader in Providing Incorporation Services
www.bizfilings.com

Uncommon Spaces
Retail Setup Suggestions
http://retailtrafficmag.com

About Retail Industry
Inventory Management Solutions
http://retailindustry.about.com

Microsoft Business Solutions
Retail Management System
https://mbs.microsoft.com
(888) 477-7989

FRANCHISE

Creative Memories
www.creativememories.com

SCRAPBOOKING MAGAZINES

Craftrends Magazine
www.craftrends.com

Ivy Cottage Creations/Creative Express!
1-800-563-8679
www.creativexpress.com

PaperKuts magazine
www.paperkuts.com

Scrap Easy Online Magazine
www.scrapeasy.com

Simple Scrapbooks Magazine
www.simplescrapbooksmag.com

Stuck on the Edge
www.stuckontheedge.com

Your Creative Spirit/*Creative Paper Crafts Online Magazine*
www.yourcreativespirit.com

Memory Makers
12365 Huron St. Suite 500
Denver, CO 80234-3488
(303) 452-0048

SUCCESSFUL HOME-BASED SCRAPPERS

Sharon Colasuonno, Senior Unit Leader
Creative Memories
www.creativememories.com/sharoncolasuonno

Suzi Moran
Creative Memories
www.creativememories.com/SuziMoran

Susie Monaro
Creative Memories
www.creativememories.com/SusieMonaro

Kelli Rice
Creative Memories
www.creativememories.com/KelliRice

Brandi Ginn
Scrapbook writer and illustrator for magazines and books.
nginn@mstar2.net

Index

Books from Allworth Press

Allworth Press is an imprint of Allworth Communications, Inc. Selected titles are listed below.

How to Start of Faux Painting or Mural Business
by Rebecca Pittman (paperback, 6 × 9, 208 pages, $19.95)

Selling Your Crafts, Revised Edition
by Susan Joy Sager (paperback, 6 × 9, $19.95, 288 pages)

Creating a Successful Crafts Business
by Rogene A. Robbins and Robert Robbins (paperback, 6 × 9, 256 pages, $19.95)

Crafts and Craft Shows: How to Make Money
by Philip Kadubec (paperback, 6 × 9, 208 pages, $16.95)

Business and Legal Forms for Crafts
by Tad Crawford (paperback, 8 × 11, 176 pages, $19.95)

The Law (in Plain English)® for Crafts
by Leonard DuBoff (paperback, 6 × 9, 224 pages, $18.95)

The Fine Artist's Guide to Marketing and Self-Promotion, Revised Edition
by Julius Vitali (paperback, 6 × 9, 256 pages, $19.95)

How to Grow as an Artist
by Daniel Grant (paperback, 6 × 9, 240 pages, $16.95)

Legal Guide for the Visual Artist, Fourth Edition
by Tad Crawford (paperback, 8 × 11, 272 pages, $19.95)

The Business of Being an Artist, Third Edition
by Daniel Grant (paperback, 6 × 9, 352 pages, $19.95)

The Artist's Complete Health and Safety Guide, Third Edition
By Monona Rossol (paperback, 6 × 9, 416 pages, $24.95)

Licensing Art & Design, Revised Edition
by Caryn R. Leland (paperback, 6 × 9, 128 pages, $16.95)

Please write to request our free catalog. To order by credit card, call 1-800-491-2808 or send a check or money order to Allworth Press, 10 East 23rd Street, Suite 210, New York, NY 10010. Include $5 for shipping and handling for the first book ordered and $1 for each additional book. Ten dollars plus $1 for each additional book if ordering from Canada. New York State residents must add sales tax.

If you would like to see our complete catalog on the World Wide Web, you can find us at **www.allworth.com.**